# Avril Lavigne

## Celebrity with Heart

Jeff Burlingame

**Enslow Publishers, Inc.**
40 Industrial Road
Box 398
Berkeley Heights, NJ  07922
USA

http://www.enslow.com

**Library of Congress Cataloging-in-Publication Data**

Burlingame, Jeff.
 Avril Lavigne : celebrity with heart / Jeff Burlingame.
   p. cm. — (Celebrities with heart)
 Includes bibliographical references and index.
 Summary: "A biography of Canadian rock singer Avril Lavigne"—Provided by publisher.
 ISBN 978-0-7660-3407-5
 1. Lavigne, Avril—Juvenile literature. 2. Singers—Canada—Biography—Juvenile
literature. I. Title.
 ML3930.L25B87 2011
 782.42166092—dc22
 [B]
                            2009023808

052010 Lake Book Manufacturing, Inc., Melrose Park, IL

Printed in the United States of America

10 9 8 7 6 5 4 3 2 1

**To Our Readers:** We have done our best to make sure all Internet addresses in this book
were active and appropriate when we went to press. However, the author and publisher
have no control over and assume no liability for the material available on those Internet sites
or on other Web sites they may link to. Any comments or suggestions can be sent by e-mail
to comments@enslow.com or to the address on the back cover.

Every effort has been made to locate all copyright holders of material used in this book.
If any errors or omissions have occurred, corrections will be made in future editions of this book.

♻ Enslow Publishers, Inc., is committed to printing our books on recycled paper. The
paper in every book contains 10% to 30% post-consumer waste (PCW). The cover board
on the outside of each book contains 100% PCW. Our goal is to do our part to help young
people and the environment too!

**Illustration Credits:** Associated Press, pp. 1, 4, 7, 8, 13, 15, 25, 37, 41, 48, 52, 59, 62, 68,
79, 85, 94; Everett Collection, Inc., pp. 19, 31, 71, 74, 91.

**Cover Illustration:** Associated Press.

# Contents

Avril Lavigne

# A Royal Performance

This was a special invitation. It was the kind of invitation that makes people scream for joy when they receive it. It was the kind of invitation people tell their children and grandchildren about—a story so grand it never stops being told, in fact. The invitation was for a date to perform for a prince. July 11, 2004, was to be Avril Lavigne's big day.

Lavigne's invitation came from England's Prince Charles, who had placed the Canadian singer on his list of performers for his Party in the Park charity concert in London. Exactly why the fifty-five-year-old Prince of Wales wanted Lavigne to headline his annual event is not

known. But there is a good chance it had something to do
with his youngest son, Prince Harry.

Months before the show, a friend of Prince Harry
said, "Harry put Avril right at the top of his wish list of
performers—and it has really paid off for him. He really
likes her music and thinks she's cute. He can't wait."[1] Talks
of a potential romance between the two nineteen-year-
olds filled gossip magazines and Web sites. One headline
asked if a "Lavigne and Prince Harry Romance [is] in the
Cards?"[2] Much of the world wondered the same thing:
What would happen when the two finally met in July?

Prince Harry was not the only one eager for the day of
the concert to arrive. Some 100,000 other music fans also
could not wait for the Party in the Park. And rightfully
so. The list of performers was full of stars. In addition to
Lavigne, Natasha Bedingfield, The Corrs, Lenny Kravitz,
Alanis Morissette, Lionel Richie, and more were scheduled
to perform. Former Spice Girl Geri Halliwell was to be at
the party, too.

By the time Lavigne and her band took to the stage, the
crowd was frenzied. Lavigne had just released her second
album, which was number one in England, the United
States, and many other countries across the world. She was
one of the hottest performers on the planet.

The crowd grew crazier with each song the pigtailed
pop star performed. After her latest hit single, "My
Happy Ending," Lavigne muttered a quick "Thank you,"

as the screams of young girls rose from the crowd. Lavigne acknowledged their cries and promptly paid the arm-waving ladies back, dedicating "Don't Tell Me" to them. When Lavigne ditched her guitar, grabbed the microphone and bounced around the stage singing her smash hit, "Sk8er Boi," the crowd bounced and sang along. During the third chorus of "I'm With You," Lavigne turned the microphone around, letting the Hyde Park crowd sing the lovesick lyrics. At the end of the song, Lavigne blew a kiss to the crowd and told them to enjoy the rest of the show.

British princes William and Harry (left to right) are photographed together in July 2004. Prince Harry was rumored to be a big fan of Avril Lavigne at the time.

Prince Charles waves to the crowd as British pop star Will Young (left) applauds during the Party in the Park charity event held in London's Hyde Park on July 11, 2004.

Lavigne was supposed to enjoy the rest of the seven-hour show, too. There was even a special seat saved for her, right next to Prince Charles in the royal press box. But Lavigne did not join the prince. Hearing this, event organizers panicked, and filled the empty seat with British singer Will Young, who had performed earlier in the day. An empty seat next to the prince could not be tolerated. People would wonder what was going on.

The Party in the Park was a success. More than one million dollars was raised for the Prince's Trust, a charity that assists young people in finding work and educational opportunities. British media reported that fact, but what they were really interested in was finding out the reason Lavigne did not take her seat beside the prince. The day after the concert, the headlines were relentless. "Mean Lavigne Snubs Charles," read one.[3] "Avril Poops Party," read another.[4] Lavigne's managers said she did not sit beside the prince because she had a plane to catch. But one person who was backstage said Lavigne did not want to sit next to the prince because, "she is cripplingly shy and hates publicity stunts."[5] Lavigne never has given an official explanation. But her brief post-performance interview may have contained a clue. When asked, "Who's your type of man? Is it [actor] Stephen Dorff or is it Prince Harry?"[6] Lavigne laughed before giving her answer: "I'm into rock stars. Guys with guitars."[7]

At that, Lavigne left London the same way she had entered it: a chart-topping, rebellious teenage musician, determined to create her own story to tell her grandchildren. This is the story of how a girl from small-town Canada went on to set musical records across the world. And, most importantly, how she did it all on her own terms.

# 2

# She Was a Sk8er Girl

It did not take long for John and Judy Lavigne to realize their second child was blessed with the gift of music. To this day, Judy Lavigne can recall the exact moment she noticed Avril Ramona Lavigne's star might one day shine brighter than most people's. She said, "One day I started singing 'Jesus Loves Me,' and I couldn't believe it when she sang along."[1]

As part of a devout Baptist household, it was not surprising that Avril would know the words to a common and basic Christian hymn. What was surprising was that she would know the words to any song—since she was just two years old when she began singing it. The young parents were shocked at their daughter's ability. Her mother said, "We knew she was talented, but we didn't realize how talented."[2]

In a few years, the Lavignes would realize just how special their second child—whose first name is French for "April"—really was. But for the time being, the French-Canadian parents simply encouraged the two-year-old to continue singing. This was easy to do. Unprompted and at every opportunity, Avril would burst into song. Years later, Avril said, "I remember when I was really young, standing on my bed like it was a stage, singing at the top of my lungs and visualizing thousands of people surrounding me."[3]

Thousands of people did surround Avril when she was growing up—five thousand to be exact. That was the entire population of Napanee, Ontario, the small Canadian town the Lavignes moved to in 1989. Avril was five at the time, having begun her life journey September 27, 1984, thirty miles to the west in a somewhat larger city named Belleville. By the time the Lavignes moved to Napanee, their family was five people strong. Avril's older brother, Matthew, was seven. Her younger sister, Michelle, was two. John Lavigne worked as a technician for a phone company. Judy Lavigne was a stay-at-home mom. The religious parents regularly prayed and attended church. That is where, at age seven, Avril began singing in front of more than just her family. Her first public outing was as part of her church's choir.

Avril later said, "There was always music at the church. That's where I got my start."[4]

When she was ten, Avril moved out front of the church choir, and sang her first solo during a Christmas production. In the middle of the show, Avril stepped to the center of the stage and belted out one minute of the Christian hymn "Near to the Heart of God." Though the spotlight shining down on her petite frame dwarfed the curly-haired blonde who was dressed like an angel, Avril was not at all nervous.

Avril's singing began to blossom after her successful church solo. Soon, she sang anywhere in public that would have her. In rural Ontario, that generally meant performing at county fairs and other smaller talent competitions. Generally, Avril would perform karaoke style, singing over the top of the backing track of songs from her favorite artists. Those favorite artists included current country stars such as LeAnn Rimes, the Dixie Chicks, and Faith Hill. It was a far cry from the style of music Avril later would become known for. But at the time, country and religious music were the only styles she had ever heard.

Located some one hundred miles northeast of Canada's largest city, Toronto, Napanee is home to one of Goodyear's largest tire manufacturing plants and Gibbard Furniture Shops, Canada's oldest furniture store, founded around 1835. Life in Napanee was exactly as it is in many small towns across the rest of Canada and the United States:

Avril Lavigne proudly displays the Canadian flag pinned to the back of her sweatshirt as she arrives at the MuchMusic Video Awards in Toronto, Canada, on June 17, 2007. Lavigne was raised in a small town in Canada.

slow-paced and often sports-oriented. Avril's brother, Matt, was very much into the latter, and Avril frequently followed in his footsteps. Avril said, "If he played hockey, I had to play hockey. He played baseball, I wanted to."[5]

And so she did both. She took to the frozen pond in the family's backyard as frequently as possible during the winter to practice her hockey skills. The practice paid off. Avril joined an all-boy's hockey league and excelled, twice winning the most valuable player award. Fights are common in the sport of hockey, and Avril got into her share of them. She even started some. Her dad said, "One time, the two teams were coming off the ice and next thing you know there's a great big commotion and moms and dads were pulling kids out. I went to the dressing room thinking, 'Who's that rotten kid that started this?' and turns out some guy called one of Avril's teammates fat pig or something and Avril slugged him right in the mask. So she started it."[6] She always was small in stature, but Avril never was afraid to stand up to anyone.

Avril's wish to play baseball like her older brother also came true, and she began pitching for a local baseball team. Other outdoor activities were among Avril's favorite things to do. She would go camping, dirt bike riding, and four-wheeling. Years later, Avril would address exactly what her small-town life was like growing up, in a song she wrote called "My World." In it, she talked about what she did for fun in Napanee, including how she beat the boys up and never wore much makeup. The song's lyrics perfectly matched what she told one interviewer. She said, "I'm just not a girlie girl."[7] Anyone who had been around Avril knew that to be true. Especially those boys she picked fights with.

Avril attended Westdale Park Public School but her mother transferred her to Cornerstone Christian Academy in the fourth grade. The just-opened Cornerstone was a private school located at the site of the Lavigne family's church, the Evangel Temple. When she graduated from Cornerstone, Avril received two awards, including the Marie Cowling Memorial Award for having "a musical ability out

Youngsters play hockey on the frozen Rideau Canal in Ottawa, Ontario, Canada, as part of the Hockey Day in Canada festivities held on February 19, 2005. Like many kids in Canada, Avril Lavigne enjoyed playing ice hockey.

**15**

of a heart for ministry and a desire to serve others," and the Robbie Lakins Award for Most Improved Graduate.[8] She also continued her athletic endeavors at Cornerstone, and set a triple jump record at an annual track meet.

After leaving Cornerstone, Avril moved on to the much-larger Napanee District Secondary School. Her behavior there took a turn for the worse. She began hanging out with the skater kids and often got suspended or kicked out of classes for misbehaving. In tenth grade, she even learned to skateboard herself.

One constant positive in Avril's life was music. She had never stopped performing. Her musical career really began to take off when she turned fourteen. At that point, Avril was involved with the Lennox Community Theatre. She had appeared as Sally in the play *You're a Good Man, Charlie Brown,* and also performed in a couple of other plays there. Local folksinger Stephen Medd spotted Lavigne during one of those plays and thought she might be a good fit to sing on some of the songs on a new album he was recording. Shortly afterwards, Lavigne accompanied Medd, who also was a friend of the family, into a recording studio in the nearby city of Kingston. It was Avril's first time inside a studio, but she immediately felt at home there. So at home, in fact, that she recorded many of her vocals in one take. Medd said, "This is a 14-year-old girl, never been in a studio, walks in like a pro and nailed it. It completely stunned me."[9]

Avril sang on several of Medd's songs, including "Touch the Sky," and "World to Me." Avril's dad even played bass guitar on the album, titled *Quinte Spirit* after the region of Ontario located on the Bay of Quinte, where the cities of Belleville and Napanee are situated. Some proceeds from Medd's record went to benefit the Quinte Spirit Festival, held each year in Napanee. Avril and Medd performed together at the festival. In 2000, Avril sang on two more of Medd's songs—"Two Rivers" and "Temple of Life"—on his next album, *My Window to You*.

Her work on the *Quinte Spirit* CD was one of several breaks Avril got that helped jumpstart her professional career. An even bigger break came in early 1999, when Avril entered a contest sponsored by an Ottawa radio station. The grand prize was impressive. Whoever won the contest would get to sing on stage with Shania Twain when she came to perform at the Corel Centre in Ottawa. The country star was one of Avril's heroes, so the teenager quickly recorded herself singing one of Twain's songs and sent it in. She won the contest, and was flown to Ottawa for the show, which was held March 17. When Avril stepped onstage to sing "What Made You Say That?" with her idol, she said it became obvious music was the career path she would be pursuing. She later told a magazine, "As soon as I walked out in front of 20,000 people, I'd never smiled so much in my life—it was like perma-smile. And I thought, 'This is what I'm going to do with my life, walk out on stage, have my own band, and be doing my own concert with my own songs.' I'm serious—this was meant to happen to me."[10]

Another big break came in November at the Chapters bookstore in Kingston. Avril, now fifteen years old, was there signing karaoke-style covers of her favorite country songs, such as Trisha Yearwood's version of "How Do I Live" and Faith Hill's "It Matters to Me." The audience was small, but one important person was part of it. His name was Cliff Fabri.

Fabri was in charge of a Kingston-based company called RomanLine Entertainment, and had worked with several musicians. He wanted to add Lavigne to his list of clients. He said, "I saw a karaoke singer, singing new country. That's where she grew up so that's all she ever really knew. But what I saw was just a beautiful kid and that eye contact . . . the confidence . . . the way she looked at the audience and the way she dealt with the people."[11] Most importantly, it was Avril's mindset that sold him on her. He said, "I liked her voice, and obviously the looks. But it was the attitude. . . . I said to her one time, 'What about when a little doe [a baby deer] comes out and starts nudging up to the mother? What do you do?'"[12] Avril made the sound of a loud shotgun blast and answered: "Dinner!"[13]

Fabri quickly signed on to be Avril's manager. He had big plans for the singer, but it did not involve the type of

Country star Shania Twain was one of Avril Lavigne's idols when she was growing up.

songs she had been singing most of her life. Fabri pictured Avril as a rock and roll singer. He said, "'I was thinking of her as another Sheryl Crow. They both had the same small-town roots. Then I was thinking Fiona Apple, because of her independence. She definitely had attitude. So my line was Sheryl Crow meets Fiona Apple."[14] It was Fabri's belief that popular music was in need of a teenager whose musical style contrasted the sounds and images of the teens ruling the airwaves at the time. Those teens included former members of Disney's Mickey Mouse Club, Christina Aguilera and Britney Spears. Both girls were singing soft-hitting pop songs like "Genie in a Bottle" and "... Baby One More Time."

Fabri believed there were plenty of music fans, especially teenagers, who wanted to hear their peers create some harder-edged rock and roll. So that is the direction he decided to take Avril's career. But there was one big problem with Fabri's plan: Avril did not know much about any type of music outside of country and gospel. Fabri said, "When we started, Avril's idea of punk was Blink-182. She didn't know who the Sex Pistols were. . . . So we worked on everything."[15] Avril said growing up in a strict religious household did not allow her to be exposed to much rock and roll. She said, "My mom wouldn't even let me sing [the country song] 'Strawberry Wine,' because it had the word 'wine' in it and I was this little kid."[16]

Fabri's work included finding ways to polish Avril's skills, and turn her into a more-seasoned performer. To do this, he had Avril perform in public as frequently as she could. He also encouraged her to work on writing her own songs, because he thought that would help make her a "career" artist, and one who would be more "real" than the manufactured Aguilera and Spears. Both of those artists had most of their songs written for them and, in many ways, were as much performers as they were musicians. By this point, Avril had spent countless hours teaching herself how to play the guitar and was on her way to becoming that true musician Fabri hoped she would become. Later in her career, Avril talked about her guitar playing. She said, "I'm not a lead guitarist . . . I'm rhythm. I will always say I'm not the greatest player, but I'm good. I love to play guitar. I use it as a writing tool and I love to play it live."[17]

Fabri put together a video of Avril performing and sent it out to people he knew in the music industry. That help was definitely important to Avril. "Making it" in the music business is extremely complex. There are many talented performers who never become successful because those who can take their careers to the next level never get to hear their music. Fabri used his connections to help Avril get her music to those people. But getting the music in front of powerful players was just one step. There was no guarantee they would react positively to what they saw and heard.

# Take Me Away

It did not take long for Fabri's plan to expose Avril to music industry insiders to pay off. The video of her he had sent to people he knew in the music industry quickly began drawing interest. Among the first to take notice was Brian Hetherman, an A&R, or artists and repertoire, director for Universal Music in Toronto. An A&R director is the person at a record label who scouts talent and helps develop that talent once it is found. Hetherman traveled to Napanee to meet with Fabri, Avril, and her family. Avril played three songs for Hetherman while he was in town, including Faith Hill's "Breathe," Sarah McLachlan's "Adia," and one of her original songs.

Hetherman said, "She had a lot of work to do, but I was really impressed. I looked at her as a little kid sister. I was really taken by her. I thought she was an absolute doll."[1]

He may have had kind words for Avril, but that did not translate into him offering her a record contract. However, Hetherman did send Avril several CDs from other artists. He thought it would help aid her growth as a musician. Hetherman believed the CDs—which included one from the pop-punk band Blink-182—would open her eyes to the different styles of music that were out there—types of music she had not been exposed to in Napanee.

Not getting a record deal did not discourage Avril or her manager. Instead, Fabri pressed on with his plan of introducing Avril to as many people and companies as he could. Nettwerk Records was one such company. Fabri had worked with the popular independent record label in the past, and sent them the videotape he had put together of Avril's performance. Nettwerk's vice president, Mark Jowett, was impressed with what he saw. Jowett met with Fabri, Avril, and her parents at the North by Northeast Music and Film Festival and Conference in Toronto, Ontario. North by Northeast is a large yearly gathering of music industry professionals, established and not-so-established musicians, and fans. A similar event called South by Southwest is held each year in the United States. Many business deals are made at both events, and record executives often discover new talent there.

Jowett did not sign Avril, either, but he did schedule her to travel to New York City to work with producer and songwriter Peter Zizzo. Zizzo had a solid reputation in the industry, having worked with popular artists such as Jennifer Lopez and Celine Dion. Zizzo remembered first seeing Avril's videotape. He said, "She was, like, fourteen and wearing these fuzzy bunny slippers, and she had a bandanna around her head."[2]

That childlike image did not deter Zizzo from wanting to work with Avril. So the young singer began making regular trips to New York to do so. During one such trip, she met with Ken Krongard, an A&R representative from Arista Records whom she had first met at the North by Northeast festival. Krongard was impressed with Avril and told his boss, Antonio "L. A." Reid, about her. Reid's reputation in the music industry was enormous. He had won three Grammy Awards and had worked with some of the biggest stars, including Toni Braxton, TLC, Whitney Houston, Usher, and Pink. Reid was interested in seeing Avril for himself, and met her at Zizzo's studio. There, Avril performed three songs for Reid—including one she helped write called "Why"—in a private showcase. After the showcase, Avril wondered how she had done. Reid thanked Avril and left the studio, but later sent a limousine to pick her and Fabri up to take them to the World Trade Center for dinner. It was there that the good news was presented. Avril said Reid told her, "you have one of the

Music industry mogul Antonio "L.A." Reid was so impressed with Avril Lavigne after hearing her perform for the first time, he signed her to a two-record deal almost immediately.

best voices I've heard . . . and that day, he was, like, 'That's it, I'm giving you a record deal.' All I knew was . . . this was really cool, I'm gonna make a record!"[3]

Actually, the deal Avril signed with Arista was for *two* records, and was worth $1.25 million. The label made a big investment in someone who had never recorded an album. But Reid was confident he had made the right decision. He said, "It was her voice and her songwriting. And she's a dynamite-looking girl with an amazing attitude."[4]

The teen's attitude soon shone through. With the blessing of her parents, Avril dropped out of high school and moved into an apartment Arista provided for her in New York City's culturally diverse Greenwich Village. Her mother said she told Avril to take correspondence classes so she could get her high school diploma. But Avril did not want to. Her mother said, "When she first got her record contract, we encouraged her to take correspondence and she was totally against it. Now it doesn't really matter."[5]

To help protect her from all the perils living in a huge city might bring to a teenager, Avril's older brother, Matt, moved to New York with her. New York City provided an exciting opportunity for Avril. But it also turned out to be a frustrating time. Her record label had visions of her singing new country songs, much like the music she had grown up listening to and what she always had performed. Those were what Reid had seen her sing when he signed her. So those were the type of songs Arista was providing her to work with when she got to New York. But those songs were not working for the stubborn sixteen year old. Neither were her co-writers. After a few months of back and forth between Fabri, Avril, and the record label, it was obvious that coming to New York City had been a bad move. Avril said, "I started working with these really talented people but the songs weren't representative of me. They started to talk about having people write for me but I had to write myself. I had to do my music. . . . I wanted to rock out."[6]

Still confident in Avril and her abilities, Arista allowed her to move to Los Angeles to get a fresh start and begin working with new people. Her first songwriting partner there was Cliff Magness, a Grammy Award-winning producer and songwriter who had worked with Celine Dion, Amy Grant, and many other stars. Magness had helped create several hit songs over the years. He and Avril immediately clicked. Magness agreed early on that he would allow Avril the freedom to express herself and help her move in the harder-edged direction she and Fabri wanted her to go in. Magness said, "The first day she came over, she was very unhappy with the way some of her writing sessions had gone. The style that was being pursued for her was country and not at all what she had in mind. At our first meeting, I asked her what she liked, musically, what some of her influences were. She mentioned Alanis Morissette and the Goo Goo Dolls. The first song we wrote was 'Unwanted.' I basically incorporated the two styles into a new direction for her. She wrote most of the lyric. I wanted her to write the lion's share of the lyric so she could express herself."[7] The duo wrote several songs together, five of which would eventually end up on Avril's first album. Magness also produced a sixth song, "Naked," that would eventually be included on that album as well.

Magness said the practice of writing songs with Avril was an equal partnership. He said, "Avril and I wrote the songs together. It was an extremely supportive and equally collaborative effort. Avril came into my studio wanting to rock and she did."[8] Magness continued, "My point of view was this: What did I know about being a [teenage] female artist from eastern Ontario living and working in New York and Los Angeles with no one to answer to but herself and her record company? . . . Her lyrics *needed* to come from her. I helped her with some grammatical issues, but the subjects and the text was all Avril."[9] Lavigne quickly fell in love with the songs she and Magness had created.

Arista next hooked Avril up with a songwriting trio called the Matrix. Made up of husband-and-wife team Graham Edwards and Lauren Christy, and Scott Spock, the Matrix members were all musicians who had decided to ditch their own performing careers to write songs for others. Avril's connection with the Matrix was not as immediate as it was with Magness. But it was not the songwriting team's fault. They had been told Avril was going to sing new country songs. So that is what they had written for her. But when they played the music for Avril, they found that the teen was less than impressed. Christy said, "She came to our studio and the record company was looking for Faith Hill-type songs, but she didn't seem to be into that at all. So we said, 'What do you want to do?' She said, 'I'm 16. I want to rock out.'"[10] So rock out is what they did. That afternoon, Avril and the Matrix wrote an edgy pop-rock song called "Complicated," which would go on to become the first single off Avril's debut album. Avril said writing the song came easily: "Graham sat down with the guitar and was, like, 'Listen to this little idea I have,' and I was like, 'Oh cool,' and then me and Lauren started singing to it. And we just recorded the guitar part and then went and laid on a blanket in the sun and wrote lyrics to it, Lauren and I."[11] The team wrote four more songs together, including another future hit, "Sk8er Boi."

Around this time, Avril fired Fabri, and hired Nettwerk Management to manage her career. Avril and her parents thought Nettwerk—with its solid reputation and vast resources and connections—would be better equipped than Fabri to handle Avril's career as it continued to grow. Nettwerk CEO Terry McBride became Avril's new manager. Fabri negotiated a monetary settlement, but it still was a bitter split. Over the years, Fabri has said he feels he was not given as much credit for Avril's success as he should have been, especially because he is the one who made her stick with the edgy image and sound that eventually came to make her rich and famous. Fabri also started saying that Avril's image was created by the record label, just as it was for the Britney Spears-type singers Avril supposedly was rebelling against. Fabri said, "The expectations now are that she's this [rebel], smashing her guitar in a slick video. That's as programmed as anything else, and it's such teenybopper-trying-to-be-cool stuff. She's not a punk. She's probably more contrived than Britney [Spears] ever was. Avril has the potential to be real, but right now, she's a poseur. Admitting you had a lot of help on your first record—that's real."[12]

Even the members of the Matrix eventually claimed that Avril had done very little writing on the five songs they worked on together. In 2003, Christy told *Rolling Stone* magazine, "With those songs, we conceived the ideas on guitar and piano. Avril would come in and sing a few melodies, change a word here or there. She came up with a couple of things in 'Complicated,' like, instead of 'Take off your stupid clothes,' she wanted it to say 'preppy clothes.'"[13] Avril quickly fought back against Christy's comments. She said when she read them, "I wanted to cry. When you create something, and someone takes that away from you, it's like [they're taking away] your baby. Lauren [Christy] and I would sing melodies and write lyrics together in the backyard on the blanket under an orange tree, and we had a great time. It was like a family. But . . . they said some

Avril Lavigne at the 2007 Teen Choice Awards. Throughout her career, Lavigne often finds herself criticized for her personal style and image.

things and burned a bridge. I'm the biggest thing that ever happened to them, so they basically [screwed] themselves over."[14]

Fabri and the Matrix are not alone in calling Avril a poseur. Over the years, several people—music industry professionals and fans alike—have said Avril's music and image is contrived. Still others say the teen's switch to preferring rock-and-roll music to country simply was a product of growing up and experiencing different kinds of music, which is what A&R man Hetherman had hoped to accomplish months earlier when he had mailed her several different types of CDs to listen to. People change their tastes every day, especially when those people are teenagers from small Canadian towns, away from home for the first time and living in New York City and Los Angeles.

With Avril, the taste changes were not only related to her brand of music. She also changed her fashion style, going from the semi-conservative dresses and blue jeans she wore in Napanee, to the more-traditional punk attire of black T-shirts and baggy pants.

Whether she was real or simply a creation of those far more powerful than her, the "new" Avril was about to be released to a worldwide audience. The most pressing question was, would there even be an audience waiting for the unknown teenage singer?

# Her World

So-called manufactured acts ruled popular music in the spring of 2002. Those groups included "boy bands," such as the Backstreet Boys and 'N Sync, and teenage girls, such as Christina Aguilera and Britney Spears. Their music was called "manufactured" because the artists singing it played minor parts, if any, in its creation. Still, music fans—mostly teens and preteens, and frequently girls—bought those artists' albums by the millions. But there were equal or greater numbers of teens that despised those acts—teens who wanted their music to be "real" and created by an artist who they believed was just as real. They did not want the glitz and glamour. They wanted rough and tumble. They wanted someone less polished and preppy. Someone they felt was more like them.

When Avril's first record, *Let Go,* hit stores on June 4, 2002, music fans across the world had what they were looking for, although they might not have known it at first. That is because the album's first single, "Complicated," was a little lighter than most of the songs on the seventeen-year-old Canadian's spunky album. Lyrically, however, "Complicated" showed the public exactly what they would be getting from Avril. The song's lyrics talked about the teen's disdain for those who pretend to be one type of person around certain people and a completely different person around others. In an interview, Avril described what the song was about. She said, "I was fed up with people being two-faced and phony. It can be a boyfriend or a friend or people you work with. So many people act like they're somebody else. Sometimes when I'm with a guy alone, you'll look into each other's eyes and everything's awesome. Then, when you're around his friends, he treats you like crap. That's what that song's about: People being fake. I hate that so much."[1]

The addictive song was an immediate smash hit, with radio stations across the world putting it into heavy rotation almost as soon as they received it. Soon, Avril's

> **"People being fake. I hate that so much."**

voice was everywhere, reminding older listeners of a young Alanis Morissette and thrilling younger listeners who were hearing the style of music from a teen for the first time.

"Complicated" quickly became a top single in both the United States and Canada. The song dragged Avril's debut album along with it to the top. Young fans were eating her music up, but professional critics gave Avril's debut album mixed reviews. Naysayers called the singer contrived, too. But nothing seemed to be able to stop Avril's momentum.

Within two months, *Let Go* went double platinum, having sold more than 2 million copies. Within six months of its release, the album had sold more than 8 million copies worldwide. The showing would be considered outstanding for a vast majority of artists, many who work their entire careers and never see that kind of success. But this was just the beginning for Avril. No one knew where her ceiling was, but everyone agreed it was extremely high.

The video for "Complicated" helped establish Avril as the "anti-Britney Spears." Whereas Spears often could be seen parading around in tight, revealing outfits, Avril's choice of attire was much more understated. In the "Complicated" video, that meant tank tops and baggy pants, with an oversized tie draped around her neck. The video begins with five-foot-one-inch Avril skateboarding into the shot to ask her band members if they would like to go to the mall. Silly antics ensue, interspersed with scenes of Lavigne and her band playing the song live in a skate park. The video, directed by brothers Emmett and Brendan Malloy, won Avril an MTV Video Music Award for Best New Artist in a Video. The song won the same award at MTV's Latin American Video Music Awards. Lavigne admitted to being a bit overwhelmed at the U.S. awards ceremony, where she wore large camouflage pants, a white tank top, a striped tie, and studded bracelets. Years later, she said, "That was the first time I walked on a red carpet and everyone was freaking out and screaming my name. I don't look back and go, 'What was I thinking?' I look back and go, '... I look cool!'"[2] She also said it was the first time she felt she had really made it as a singer: "It was special because it was my first award, and because I had always watched the award shows and seen people up there winning awards, and then I would go up to my bedroom and pretend I had won one. I always thought about what it would be like ... and then when I was walking up there to accept my first award, I was like Wow, I can't believe this is happening."[3]

"Complicated" was not just appealing to teens. Many adults also enjoyed the song's catchy hooks. That fact helped the song become a crossover hit, meaning it was popular with more than one type of listener. Lavigne said there is an easy explanation for that connection: "The image of me that's out there is real. It's not like my record label made me up. I write my own songs, and when I'm

Avril Lavigne strikes a wild pose with her trophy after winning in the Best New Artist category for her video for "Complicated" at the 2002 MTV Video Music Awards.

in front of a camera, I don't try to act like something or someone I'm not."[4] "Complicated" eventually peaked at number two on the *Billboard* singles chart and hit number one on two lesser charts. The song was even parodied by humorous singer "Weird Al" Yankovic on his 2003 album *Poodle Hat*. He begins his hilarious version of Lavigne's song by singing about becoming "constipated" after eating too much pizza. Yankovic's album went on to win a Grammy Award in 2003 for Best Comedy Album.

Many called Lavigne's image and music "skate punk." In most ways, it was the exact opposite of the image most teen performers were portraying at the time. As if it were necessary, the second single off *Let Go* drove home that skate punk image. The song was called "Sk8er Boi," (pronounced "Skater Boy") and told the story of a girl who thinks she is too good for a boy who skateboards. Five years later, that boy becomes a famous rock star and the girl realizes the reason she overlooked the boy in the first place—based on what he looked like and what her friends thought—was not a very good one. To top it off, the girl is at home taking care of her baby and watching television, when she sees him on MTV.

The "Sk8er Boi" video features a concert on a city street with Lavigne singing on the hood of a car with a crowd rocking out around her. The singer's fashion choice for the shoot: spiked, studded bracelets, baggy pants, Converse shoes, and a green-and-gold T-shirt from an elementary school in North Carolina. Proving just how big a star Avril Lavigne had become in a short period of time, that school was flooded with requests from people who wanted to buy the shirt after it appeared in the video. Lavigne had bought the shirt in a thrift store in New York City.[5] A similar situation occurred a few months later, when Lavigne wore a shirt from her old soccer team on the hit TV show *Saturday Night Live,* in January 2003. The team's sponsor, Home Hardware Napanee, found its name broadcast to millions of viewers and suddenly received hundreds of requests for the shirt.

In addition to "Complicated" and "Sk8er Boi," two more singles were released from *Let Go*. They included the contemplative ballad "I'm With You," and the album's rocking opener, "Losing Grip," the song that Lavigne repeatedly has said is her favorite on the album. The album, by the way, almost had a different name. Label boss L. A. Reid thought the album should be named after one of its songs, "Anything But Ordinary." But Lavigne had other ideas, and told Reid as much. She called him and said, "Dude, I don't want to name it that. Can I just name it 'Let Go?'"[6] Reid said that was fine with him, and the name of the album was settled.

The success of *Let Go* lasted well into 2003 and even into 2004. At the 2003 Grammy Awards, Lavigne garnered five nominations. "Complicated" was nominated for Best Female Pop Vocal Performance and Song of the

Year (an honor shared with the Matrix). "Sk8er Boi" was nominated for Best Rock Vocal Performance–Female. *Let Go* was nominated for Best Pop Vocal Album, and Lavigne was nominated for Best New Artist.

Lavigne did not win in any of the five categories, but being nominated for a Grammy was an incredible accomplishment, regardless. So was performing on the show, playing "Sk8er Boi" in front of millions of viewers who were watching at home on TV. Those viewers included people attending a party in her honor at her old school in Napanee. The following year, "I'm With You" was nominated for Song of the Year–Songwriter (another honor shared with the Matrix), "Losing Grip" was nominated for Best Rock Vocal Performance–Female, and Lavigne was nominated for Best Female Pop Vocal Performance.

Lavigne did not win a Grammy in 2004 either. But that did not mean she suffered from a shortage of awards. Internationally, they came often, especially in her home country. At Canada's 2003 Juno Awards, she won New Artist of the Year, Album of the Year, Pop Album of the Year, and Single of the Year for "Complicated."

For Lavigne, the Juno Awards ceremony was a bit of a trip down memory lane. It was held at the Corel Centre in Ottawa, the same place she had sang four years earlier with Shania Twain, who was host of the 2003 event. Lavigne also performed at the award ceremony. Twain introduced

Lavigne performs "Sk8er Boi" at the 2003 Grammy Awards show.

Lavigne and her band. She said, "Back when we were on tour in 1999, I organized a talent contest in every city that we visited. The winner from each city got to come up and join me on stage to sing one of my songs . . . on opening night, right here at the Corel Centre, guess who walked out to a packed house full of confidence and proceeded to knock everybody out with her performance?"[7] Twain showed the audience a picture of the fourteen-year-old Lavigne from that night in 1999, then continued, "She's holding a picture of me, which is very cool, because here I am four years later on the very same stage holding a picture of her. How cool! . . . Today she is one of the most popular singers in the world."[8] The last part of Twain's statement was especially true. Among other honors, Lavigne also won awards in Ireland, Asia, at the World Music Awards, and at Nickelodeon's Kids' Choice Awards.

Touring generally plays a huge role in the success of an artist. Traveling from city to city creates media opportunities, helps sell merchandise, and allows fans to see in person the artist behind the music they have come to enjoy. But in Lavigne's case, her enormous success came without once hitting the road for anything other than promotional opportunities. That was due in large part to the success of her songs on the radio and the frequency with which they were played on MTV, Canada's MuchMusic, and other outlets. Lavigne had proven she could sell albums without touring. But she still was anxious to begin her first tour. She said, "I know I'm going to love it. I'll get to sleep in the same bed every night [on the tour bus]. And it will just be fun being with my best friends, my band. It's going to be an amazing experience, performing every night, doing what I love."[9]

Lavigne's first chance to experience life on the road came in March 2003, when her Try to Shut Me Up Tour kicked off in Copenhagen, Denmark. After roughly twenty more midsize shows in Europe, the production made its way back to North America for a few shows in Canada, including one at the Corel Centre in Ottawa. The tour then headed south to the United States. The tour's production was enormous, with four semi-trucks needed just to carry all the stage gear and props. Backed by a four-piece band and with opening acts Gob and Simple Plan, Lavigne performed in front of several large video screens to sold-out houses, mostly consisting of preteen and teen girls and the parents that brought them there.

Seasoned adult music critics may have written mixed reviews on the eighteen-year-old's first headlining tour, but one thing is certain: the kids loved it. So much so, in fact, that tens of thousands of them paid to see—and hear—parts of it twice. Once live, and once when the audio and video footage from the sold-out tour was released in November on a live DVD/CD combination called *My World*. The release featured an entire live performance from the last show of the Try to Shut Me Up Tour, and a behind-the-scenes documentary of Lavigne. The six-song CD included Lavigne's covers of Metallica's "Fuel," Green Day's "Basket Case," and Bob Dylan's "Knockin' on Heaven's Door," in addition to live versions of "Sk8er Boi" and "Unwanted." Rounding out the CD was a studio version of Lavigne's song, "Why," which had been previously released as a B-side on the "Complicated" single. "Why," written by Lavigne and Peter Zizzo in New York, was the one original song Lavigne had played in her audition for Arista's LA Reid a couple years earlier in Zizzo's studio.

Lavigne's cover of Dylan's "Knockin' on Heaven's Door" had been recorded live when she was on tour in London. She recorded it for a special cause, the two-CD compilation, *Peace Songs*. Proceeds from *Peace Songs* went to benefit a charity called War Child, which aids children in war-torn areas. Though the album was filled with songs by many more-established stars—such as David Bowie, former Beatle Paul McCartney, and Celine Dion—Lavigne's song was chosen to be the album's first single. Her song alone raised more than a hundred thousand dollars to help remove unexploded grenades from schools in Iraq and to buy textbooks for the students who attended them.

The release of *My World* was made into a huge public event, with simultaneous screenings in November at twenty-four movie theaters in different cities across the United States. Lavigne attended the New York premiere of the DVD dressed in all black, wearing a white tank top underneath her black jacket.

In 2003, it seemed as though Lavigne's name, face, and voice were everywhere. In large part, that is because they were. The people marketing the teenage singer knew they had a hot product on their hands. They understood the old adage, "strike while the iron's hot." In the world of popular music, no iron was hotter than Lavigne's, and it was the plan of everyone around her to keep striking.

# 5

# Celebrity Pros and Cons

It may have been her infectious songs and powerful voice that thrust Avril Lavigne into the spotlight, but those were not the only things that kept her there. Her anti-Britney Spears image and model-like looks played large roles in that. Regardless of whether they liked her music, many men found Lavigne attractive, and her photos graced the covers of several magazines. The March 2003 cover of *Rolling Stone,* for example, showed Lavigne wearing a tight black tank top and short skirt combination that revealed her midriff. Beside her, the cover line read, "On the hunt with the Britney Slayer." Readers of the men's lifestyle magazine *FHM* voted Lavigne one of their "100 Sexiest Women in the World." Another men's magazine,

*Maxim,* named her one of its "Hot 100." Such publicity may have had nothing to do with Lavigne's music, but it helped keep her in the public eye.

Being the focus of so much publicity also brought negative attention to Lavigne, much of which she could have done without. One such issue was a rumored romance with Fred Durst, a much-older singer from the band Limp Bizkit. Durst and Lavigne met backstage during the taping of a Metallica tribute show for MTV. When Lavigne told Durst she wanted a hamburger, he had someone go out and get her a whole box of them. A short time later, Durst showed up at one of Lavigne's concerts wearing a T-shirt that read, "I (heart) Avril."[1] But Lavigne, then nineteen, wanted nothing to do with the thirty-three-year-old Durst. Lavigne told *Rolling Stone* magazine, "He was disappointed that I wouldn't even go near him. He was a little [angry] that I went to my room alone that night."[2] Durst later denied doing many of the things Lavigne said he did.

Lavigne also began a feud with fellow teen singer Hilary Duff in 2003. The feud began when Duff told an interviewer she thought Lavigne should appreciate her fans more. Lavigne, apparently, had told fans who copied the way she dressed to get a life. Lavigne told Duff to mind her own business. The Duff–Lavigne rivalry continued for a while, although most reports say it finally has ended.

While the Durst and Duff incidents were basically harmless celebrity feuds, some situations Lavigne's celebrity brought upon her were frightening, especially one that started in early 2003. That is when a thirty-year-old Washington state man named James Speedy began sending Lavigne, her family, and her managers letters,

Avril Lavigne covers the song "Fuel" during a taping of a Metallica tribute show for MTV on May 3, 2003.

e-mails, flowers, and bottles of wine. That summer, Speedy flew to Ontario and was arrested by Canadian police across the street from Lavigne's parents' home in Napanee.[3] The police sent him back to the United States. Speedy was again arrested nearly a year later as a precaution because he had e-mailed Lavigne's manager hours before the singer was about to hold a concert near where Speedy lived. Police searched Speedy's home and found three guns, along with songs and letters addressed to Lavigne. Speedy was charged with stalking. At his court sentencing, he told the judge, "I just wanted to meet Avril Lavigne. I'm not in love with her. I didn't want to hurt her."[4] The judge gave Speedy thirty days in jail and a five-hundred-dollar fine, and placed him under court supervision for two years.[5]

Lavigne did not let the negative events in her life deter her from remaining positive and trying to help those that needed it. When the Canadian city of Toronto suffered from an outbreak of the deadly Severe Acute Respiratory Syndrome, or SARS, disease in March 2003, Lavigne stepped in to help and agreed to perform at a star-studded benefit concert to help the city's struggling tourism industry. That same month, she donated a signed drum skin from her performance at a British awards show for an auction to raise money for a five-year-old boy's fight against cancer.

With all that was going on in her life, it would have been easy for Lavigne to overlook what it was that made her famous in the first place—music. Fortunately for her legions of mostly young fans, she did not let anything come between her and her songs. In fact, Lavigne decided to take her music where those young fans frequently hang out—shopping malls.

In March 2004, Lavigne began a twenty-one-city tour of U.S. malls. The two-person acoustic tour featured Lavigne and her songwriting partner and touring guitarist, Evan Taubenfeld, playing guitar and singing. The tour was called "Live and By Surprise," and was named that for a good reason. The location of each show was announced just forty-eight hours in advance. That proved to be plenty of notice for Lavigne's fans, who packed each location in spite of the short notice. Lavigne said, "We thought it would be cool to put on a free show and give back to fans. It was more than I expected. The crowds ranged from a few thousand to ten thousand. Some of [the events] were moved outside. It's been great."[6] An acoustic album featuring recordings from the tour was released later in the year.

The mall tour was part of another strategic marketing move by her record label. This one was designed to promote Lavigne's upcoming album. During the mall tour, Lavigne played three songs off *Let Go* and previewed songs from that soon-to-be-released album. One such new song, "Don't Tell Me," was to be the first single off Lavigne's second album. The single was released to radio stations while the mall tour was in progress.

The song, co-written by Taubenfeld, talked about not giving in to sexual pressures from a boy, and how it often is better just to be alone. A video was shot for the song. It begins with Lavigne and a boy sitting on her bed. As the boy gets up and begins to leave, Lavigne—dressed in a pink tank top, underwear and knee-high socks with skulls and crossbones on them—begins singing the lyrics. Then Lavigne, now dressed in all black and wearing a studded belt with silver chains dangling from it, follows the boy down the street, hauntingly singing the song to him all the while. As the song ends, the boy rounds a street corner and disappears from Lavigne's view.

Shortly after the mall tour ended in the middle of April, it was time to unveil Lavigne's second album, *Under My Skin*. Several changes had taken place in the two years since the highly successful *Let Go* had been released. Foremost among them was Lavigne's dogged determination to prove wrong those who said she was not a songwriter. To do this, she ditched the Matrix songwriting team, which had bad-mouthed her to the media, and instead co-wrote most of the album's material with Taubenfeld and singer-songwriter Chantal Kreviazuk.

A fellow Canadian, Kreviazuk was married to Raine Maida, the singer of another Canadian band called Our Lady Peace. That band had opened for Lavigne on her first tour, so the thirty-one-year-old Kreviazuk had known the nineteen-year-old Lavigne for a while before beginning to write songs with her. When they did begin to write, the pair clicked almost immediately. Lavigne said, "We became really good friends, and no one knew we were writing together. Every single night for two weeks, we would write a new song. And then I was like, 'OK, I'm ready to record them.'"[7]

Six of those songs—written at Kreviazuk's and Maida's house in California—made it onto the final album, as

Lavigne performs at the Southwest Plaza Mall in Littleton, Colorado, on April 14, 2004.

did three Lavigne had written with Taubenfeld, and one written with Ben Moody, a former member of the popular rock band Evanescence. Moody and Lavigne had been friends for a while. One time, he and Lavigne had even got matching star tattoos on their wrists.

Unlike the Matrix, *Let Go* songwriter Cliff Magness did return to work with Lavigne on her second album. None of the songs the pair wrote together made it onto *Under My Skin,* but two eventually were released. The first, "I Always Get What I Want," was included on the soundtrack to the movie *The Princess Diaries 2: Royal Engagement.* The second, "Take It," was used as the B-side for a future single.

Magness said he noticed Lavigne had changed since he had first worked with her two years before. He said, "She had developed a more opinionated and involved persona. She wanted more control artistically, which is pretty common for sophomore artists."[8] Lavigne agreed. She said, "With the new album I've changed and grown. I'm a really deep person and in touch with myself and my feelings. You can tell I'm older. I think, lyrically, I've kind of stepped up a notch."[9]

By this point, *Let Go* had sold 14 million copies worldwide. Whether those millions of Lavigne fans would take that journey with her remained to be seen.

# On the Road Again

**A**fter months of prerelease promotion—including the successful U.S. mall tour and appearances on "Late Night With David Letterman," "Live With Regis & Kelly," and at the Nickelodeon Kids' Choice Awards—*Under My Skin* finally was made available to the public on May 25, 2004.

Lavigne's decision to take more control over all aspects of the album was almost immediately vindicated. *Under My Skin* debuted as the top-selling album in the United States, with nearly four hundred thousand copies sold in its first week. Those sales numbers were larger than any week *Let Go* had experienced.[1] And that album had sold millions of copies in just two years. Many wondered how high *Under My Skin*'s sales numbers could go, especially after it immediately went to number one in many other countries, including the singer's homeland of Canada.

The day her new album was released, an excited Lavigne took to the promotional circuit to talk about its release. During an appearance on MTV's *Total Request Live* show, Lavigne was asked what she thought of the way she was portrayed by the public and the media, which had been known to bestow labels on her like "punk" and "rebel." She said, "I just wanna say that all that stuff's really annoying, and I don't think that I'm any of those things and it's just the media and they don't even know me and they don't know what they're talking about."[2]

At that point, Lavigne turned to the camera and stuck up her middle finger. The gesture panicked those in control at the cable network. They canceled Lavigne's scheduled performance of a second song. That the act was indeed rebellious—one of the labels she had been given by the media and despised—appeared to be lost on Lavigne, who pumped her fist in the air and screamed after her obscene gesture. Throughout the years, Lavigne's middle finger flash became a common sight. She has made the gesture nearly everywhere—from red carpet events to everyday run-ins with paparazzi.

As was its singer, *Under My Skin* was also rebellious. While *Let Go* was filled with poppy, sing-along songs that sometimes featured punk-like edges to them, *Under My*

*Skin* was a bit darker, and certainly more serious. Written by Lavigne and Taubenfeld, "Take Me Away" kicks off the album with a relationship-themed bang. The pace slows down a bit for the second song, "Together," though Lavigne's multi-tracked vocals remain powerful as ever.

The album's first single, "Don't Tell Me," follows. The rest of the album runs the musical gamut. There are sensitive ballads such as "How Does It Feel" and "Forgotten." There also are up-tempo tracks, such as "My Happy Ending," which went on to become the album's most-successful single when it was released in June. The song peaked at number nine in the United States, but was a number one hit in Mexico and several Asian countries.

"Nobody's Home" was the album's third single and "Fall to Pieces" its fourth. Each of those two songs made it onto the U.S. and Canadian charts, though neither could be considered a smash hit. A fifth single, "He Wasn't," was released in some countries, but not in the United States. Perhaps the most special of the album's songs, for Lavigne in particular, was the last song, "Slipped Away." Lavigne wrote it—along with Kreviazuk—for her grandfather, who recently had died. The sad lyrics talk about Lavigne's regrets over not being able to kiss him goodbye.

It was evident early on that *Under My Skin* did not contain the monster hits of its predecessor. That kind of success is hardly ever repeated. Songs such as "Complicated" and "Sk8er Boi" were so catchy and contained such gigantic hooks that they became ingrained in the minds of even non-Lavigne fans, so many times were they played on mainstream radio, in movies, and on MTV. Minus those incessant spins from its singles, it would be difficult for *Under My Skin* to match the gigantic sales numbers of *Let Go*. And it did not. But that did not mean Lavigne's second album was unsuccessful. It was anything but.

In fact, many critics and fans thought it was even better than her first one. *Rolling Stone* gave *Under My Skin* three-and-a-half stars out of five, one half-star higher than it had given *Let Go*. The popular music magazine said: "She put together an album that's both more satisfying and more formulaic. Lavigne doesn't incorporate any new ideas on *Skin*; instead, she shines up her old ones, often multitracking her voice to make sure you don't miss the mile-wide choruses."[3]

Gone are the days where discussing a musician or band's latest record meant talking only about the songs it contained. Thanks to the video revolution, pop music stars nowadays are more of an audio *and* a visual package. For someone to be successful, not only do their songs have to be good, but their image does, too. So, with every new batch of songs comes an image makeover. Lavigne's world was no different.

Gone from the nineteen-year-old's wardrobe were the much-copied striped ties and white tank tops that had rid many a father of both his favorite neckpiece and a cheap undershirt. In their place were black T-shirts and dark makeup. Lavigne's hair was now really long and blonde. It was Lavigne with an edge—less skate punk and more preppy goth. Whether it was a maturing Lavigne or her managers that coordinated the makeover, one thing is certain: Her new look matched the darker music of *Under My Skin* just as well as her old look had matched the lighter sound of *Let Go*.

As had "Don't Tell Me," each of *Under My Skin*'s other music videos helped drive home Lavigne's darker image. For most of "My Happy Ending," Lavigne is dressed in a black tank top and a fluffy pink dress, sitting in an empty theater, singing and watching a film filled with memories of her and a former boyfriend. At the end, she straps on a guitar and joins her band outside to finish the song together on the theater's rooftop.

In "Fall to Pieces," Lavigne alternately plays herself leading an old-time band and a dingy-looking, black-haired teenager living on the streets, which is what the song's lyrics are about. The "He Wasn't" video features a simple concept of Lavigne wearing a multitude of girlish outfits singing in front of her band and acting silly.

Overall, both the album and the image of *Under My Skin* were more mature than that of *Let Go*. Lavigne had clearly grown up in the two years between the releases, and her image and music reflected that. She told one reporter, "You do a lot more growing between the ages of 16 and 19 than you do

Lavigne sports her preppy-goth look at the Maxim Hot 100 Party in New York City on May 16, 2007.

from 27 to 30. Sometimes I'm immature, but most of the time I've got a handle on things. Other people my age go to school, then pursue their career, then get a job, and I'm kind of there. I have a house. I have a job. It's like, 'What's next?'"[4]

What was next for Lavigne was another major tour, this one in support of the release of *Under My Skin*. Generally, artists tour immediately after their release hits the stores. But it took a little while longer for Lavigne's post-album tour to begin. Lavigne began her album tour in September, four months after *Under My Skin* had been released. For Lavigne's fans, the wait was worth it.

Lavigne named her tour the Bonez Tour after her love for the skull and crossbones symbol, which she has on a lot of her clothes. The tour kicked off September 26, in Munich, Germany, one day before Lavigne's twentieth birthday. After stops in France, Holland, and the United Kingdom, the tour came to North America. The first stop was October 25, in Dallas, Texas. Opening for Lavigne was singer-songwriter Butch Walker. Walker had co-written "My Happy Ending" with Lavigne, had produced *Under My Skin,* and also had played several instruments on the hit album. Previously, Walker was a member of a moderately successful band from the 1990s, Marvelous 3. The Bonez Tour spanned more than one hundred shows, and most of the major arenas in the United States and Canada. The first leg of the tour ended November 25, in Kelowna, British Columbia.

After a few months' break for the holidays, the tour resumed March 1 in Osaka, Japan. The second leg of the tour visited many of the same cities, and ended in September 2005—nearly a year to the day after it began. During the tour, Lavigne showed off her musical versatility, playing several instruments, including guitar, piano, and even drums. She told MTV doing so helped keep the tour fresh. She said, "I usually have someone like Butch Walker come out and sing and I'll play the drums. I play the piano on a bunch of songs. I do some songs by myself on acoustic guitar and then of course I play electric guitar during other songs. So I'm all over the place."[5]

The personal lives of most musicians take backseats to music when they are on the road, because tour schedules often are hectic. But somehow, Lavigne's life seemed to produce more and more news every day, regardless of what city she might be in. By the time Lavigne turned twenty, she had become more than just a rock-and-roll singer. She was a full-fledged star, magazine cover girl, and a regular in gossip magazines and related Web sites.

Lavigne had long professed to being shy, but she was not that way when it came to publicity. Lavigne often gave gossip seekers exactly what they were looking for. When singer Ashlee Simpson got caught lip-syncing a song on *Saturday Night Live,* Lavigne pounced. She told the *New York Post,* "In a way it was good because it showed that people are doing it on TV all the time. I've never

Lavigne plays guitar at the Fleet Center in Boston in November 2004. Boston was just one of the stops on her Bonez tour that year.

lip-synced once in my life . . . I never will. I'm a singer, and I sing live. That's what music is about. I see lip-syncing all the time at awards shows, and it makes me think, how sad. It's a disgrace that this is what music has come to."[6]

When asked by the same reporter to elaborate, she was quick to fuel the fire of her longtime feud with another singer. Lavigne said, "People like Hilary Duff. I've never heard her sing live. Each time I've seen her perform, she lip-synchs. She sings to tracks and they either [amplify] her vocals very low or she just doesn't sing at all. You don't deserve to be there if that's what you do."[7]

When asked about the sexy way in which Britney Spears dressed, Lavigne said she dressed like a "showgirl"[8] and added, "You won't see me on stage in a sexy outfit or my hair in ribbons. If that's what someone wants to do then so be it, but I wouldn't be seen dead looking like that."[9] When she performed at the Prince's Trust charity concert in London, but did not sit next to Prince Charles to watch part of the show as planned, it made tabloid headlines. And when things did not go her way during a photo shoot for *Maxim* magazine in Los Angeles, the angry star took matters into her own hands. She smashed bottles on the floor and wrecked some furniture. Critics may not have believed Lavigne was truly a rebellious punk rocker, but she often behaved like one. If she was acting, she was good at it.

Musical projects remained on Lavigne's radar. During a brief break on her Bonez Tour, she and producer Walker took to a studio to record a new version of the theme song to the children's TV show *SpongeBob SquarePants*. The song was to be featured in the upcoming film based on the hit cartoon. As might be expected, Lavigne's version of the forty-six-second song was more rock-and-roll than the original. She told MTV, "I made the song a little more edgy. There are a lot of loud guitars, and we picked up the tempo a little and sang it with a little more attitude."[10] In fact, the film's entire soundtrack had a harder edge than might be expected for a Nickelodeon cartoon. Other acts on the album included the Flaming Lips, Wilco, Ween, and even heavy metal legends Motörhead. The soundtrack, as was most everything related to both the sea-dwelling cartoon creature and Lavigne, was a big seller.

Lavigne's other musical adventures in 2004 included co-writing the song "Breakaway" for former *American Idol* winner Kelly Clarkson. The lyrics centered on someone from a small town who yearns to become a star. It was not a stretch to imagine Lavigne had a hand in writing them, given that the words almost perfectly matched her life's story. The song appeared on *The Princess Diaries 2: Royal Engagement* soundtrack, along with Lavigne's "I Always Get What I Want." Clarkson's version of "Breakaway" also found its way onto her debut CD of the same name. When the song was released as a single, it peaked at number three on the *Billboard* charts.

# Branching Out

When a massive earthquake and subsequent series of gigantic waves, or tsunami, hit Southeast Asia the day after Christmas 2004, more than two hundred thousand people were killed. Help to the damaged area came quickly, and from most everywhere imaginable. Governments offered millions of dollars to help aid in the recovery of the countries most hurt by the natural disasters. Average citizens across the world also gave what they could to help purchase food, drinking water, and other basic necessities for those affected. Stars from every facet of the entertainment industry also donated what they could. Lavigne was one of them.

When a tsunami-relief benefit show was scheduled for January 29 in Vancouver, British Columbia, Lavigne volunteered to perform. More than eighteen thousand people attended the four-hour-long concert, which also featured Barenaked Ladies, Sarah McLachlan, Sum 41, and other Canadian artists. More than $3 million was raised for the cause.

Shortly after the benefit concert, Lavigne joined a host of other celebrities in donating to a separate tsunami relief fund. This one was an auction held on the popular Web site eBay. Lavigne donated an autographed skateboard to that auction, and then she donated an autographed guitar to an auction for a charity, Musicians on Call, whose goal is to bring music to patients in long-term health care facilities. Lavigne donated to other charity auctions, as well, including those helping fight AIDS and cancer, and the MusiCares Foundation, which takes care of entertainers who have become sick and elderly and no longer have the means to support themselves.

Over the years, Lavigne has written several songs about boyfriends, mostly exes she now dislikes for one reason or another. Since becoming a star, however, she admitted her love life had slowed down a bit—not that it was ever on a fast pace. She said that was due in large part to her strict upbringing in small-town Canada. In 2003, Lavigne told *Rolling Stone* magazine, "I wasn't allowed to have a guy in my room. Especially not with the door shut. And [my mother] wouldn't let me call guys. They had to call me. I have that attitude now—that if a guy wants to hook up with me, he can come after me. I'm not going running after him."[1] She told the same writer what qualities her dream guy would possess. Lavigne said, "I need a guy who's sensitive. I need a guy with edge. And most importantly, a guy has to give me lots of attention and hug me all the time."[2]

Deryck Whibley must have had all those qualities and then some. Because when the singer-guitarist for Canadian pop-punk band Sum 41 asked Lavigne to marry him in June 2005, the flattered Lavigne said yes. The couple had been dating for some time, so the announcement was not a total surprise. The fact that Lavigne already had a tattoo on the inside of her right wrist of a pink heart with the letter "D" inside of it made it even less shocking. Whibley reportedly popped the question to Lavigne in Venice, Italy. Prior to dating Lavigne, Whibley had a history of public romances, most notably a high-profile one with socialite Paris Hilton.

A little more than a year after their engagement, Whibley and Lavigne wed. The outdoor ceremony took place July 15, 2006, in Montecito, California. The twenty-one-year-old bride wore a full-length strapless dress from fashion designer Vera Wang. Lavigne later told *People* magazine, "part of me was, like, I should do something cool with my wedding dress, but at the same time . . . I

Deryck Whibley and Avril Lavigne kiss during a New Year's Eve party in Las Vegas on December 31, 2007.

wanted everything to be classic. So the ceremony was very classic."[3]

The twenty-six-year-old groom wore a traditional black suit with an ivory tie that matched the color of his bride's dress. About one hundred guests attended the private ceremony, and Lavigne's father walked her down the aisle. The couple's first dance was to the song "Iris" by the Goo Goo Dolls. While the ceremony may have been "classic," the red-themed reception was anything but. Lavigne described it as "very rock and roll goth."[4] It was the same description many had given her latest public image. The newlyweds honeymooned in Italy. When they returned to the United States, they moved into a mansion in Bel Air, an upper-class section of Los Angeles, California.

At this point in her life, Los Angeles was a good place for Lavigne to be. She had been acting since her days starring in local performances in Napanee, and had professed several times to want to pursue that path in addition to what she was doing musically. Living in Los Angeles would provide her with that opportunity. Lavigne already had dabbled in the professional acting business. In 2002, Lavigne had appeared as herself in the TV show *Sabrina, the Teenage Witch,* on which she and her band played "Sk8er Boi" as the show's stars watched her. Two years later, Lavigne played herself again, this time in the teen comedy *Going the Distance.* Lavigne's songs also were featured in several movies, including the 2002 film *Sweet*

*Home Alabama* and the 2003 flick *American Wedding,* the third film in the popular *American Pie* series. "I'm With You" was featured on the soundtrack for the 2003 Jim Carrey film *Bruce Almighty.* The following year, the song won an ASCAP award for Most Performed Song from a Motion Picture.

On her love of acting, Lavigne said it all started back in Napanee. She said she, "basically started acting when I was younger. I was in the school plays, singing and stuff and then I got a record deal. The singing thing worked out. I just wanted to try it again and be creative in any way I can. I am looking forward to getting a great movie and working on a good project. . . . I make sure I am selective and careful with what I do. I have to be extra careful because I'm going to be really judged."[5] If Hollywood insiders were indeed keeping score on Lavigne's acting skills, she must have passed with flying colors.

In 2006, she was cast in two films. In the animated film *Over the Hedge,* Lavigne provided the voice for an opossum named Heather. Veteran actor William Shatner provided the voice for Ozzie, Heather's father. Many other well-known actors, including Catherine O'Hara, Nick Nolte, and Bruce Willis, also did voices for the film. The movie is an adaptation of the popular comic strip of the same name.

In the drama *Fast Food Nation,* Lavigne played a minor role as a character named Alice. In one of her scenes, she

Avril Lavigne poses with her animated counterpart, Heather, from the 2006 film, *Over the Hedge*.

even helps herd cattle. Several of Hollywood's hottest stars were also in that film, including Patricia Arquette, Ethan Hawke, Greg Kinnear, and Wilmer Valderrama. The following year, Lavigne landed another minor role as Beatrice Bell in the thriller *The Flock,* which stars Richard Gere and Claire Danes. Several reports have mentioned Lavigne possibly playing Courtney Love, the wife of Nirvana singer/songwriter Kurt Cobain, in a film about the deceased rocker. But no firm details have been set. Lavigne's name has also popped up for several other roles.

Along with her foray into acting, Lavigne also decided to give modeling a shot. To do so, she signed a contract with well-known New York City modeling agency, Ford Models. At just over five feet tall, Lavigne did not fit the typical tall-model stereotype, but felt she could do the job anyway. She said, "I want to do those really beautiful ads with the high-end products. I look through magazines and stare at ads and think, 'I'm not six feet tall, but I know I can do that.'"[6]

The move represented a big shift in thinking for a person who, just two years before, dressed in an antifashion skate-punk style. Lavigne explained this by saying, "I'm starting to feel more feminine. I'm getting into hair and make-up and image. That's the best part of being a girl."[7] Over the years, other celebrities have been Ford models, including Paris Hilton, Lindsay Lohan, and Ashley Tisdale.

Lavigne had plenty of modeling experience prior to signing with Ford. She had been on photo shoots for several magazine covers, including the April 2005 issue of popular women's magazine *Cosmopolitan,* on which she was wearing black pants and a black, stomach-revealing tank top. Other magazine covers Lavigne has graced over the years include *Rolling Stone, Seventeen, YM, Maxim,* and *Blender.* On the *Blender* cover, which was published in June 2007, Lavigne appears to be topless, with only a banner across her chest. She actually was wearing a tube top that was covered up by the magazine's banner.

That she had time to do so much was amazing, but Lavigne never neglected the one thing that put her in the position to be able to donate to charity, live in a Bel Air mansion, and pursue an acting career. That one thing was music. For now, the focus was on the music she already had created.

Lavigne kicked off 2005 by winning a Nickelodeon Kids' Choice Award for Best Female Singer. Then, when Canada's 2005 Juno Award nominees were announced, Lavigne's name appeared more times than any other person's—a whopping five times. When the awards were announced in April, Lavigne won three. She won Artist of the Year, received the Fan Choice award, and *Under My Skin* won Pop Album of the Year. She was not the only one in her household to take home a trophy. Her husband's band, Sum 41, won Rock Album of the Year for its most-recent album, *Chuck.*

The fact that Canada was proud of native-daughter Lavigne was obvious, but it became even more so in the winter of 2006. That is when the 2006 Winter Olympics held its closing ceremony in February in Turin, Italy. Because Canada was scheduled to host the 2010 Winter Olympics, the country had to make a presentation at the end of the 2006 ceremony. Lavigne was the one there representing her home country. With performers all around her, Lavigne climbed the stairs of the stage in the middle of Stadio Olimpico and sang her song "Who

Avril Lavigne, Ashley Johnson, Lou Taylor Pucci, Director Richard Linklater, and Paul Dano (left to right), on the set of *Fast Food Nation.*

Knows" to the more than thirty thousand people in attendance. When the song was over, the last piece to a large Vancouver Olympics logo made of ice was put into place, symbolizing Canada's hosting of the next Winter Olympic Games.

While her appearance at the Olympics was nothing but positive, Lavigne did see her share of negative publicity again in 2006. Most notable was her back-to-back days of spitting on paparazzi photographers—and cursing at them, too—outside a nightclub in Hollywood. Lavigne quickly released a statement apologizing for her bad behavior, which came on the day before her twenty-second birthday, September 27. She said, "It's trying at best dealing with their insistent intrusions. I meant no offense to my fans, whose relationship I truly value. I have and will always go out of my way for my fans. My behavior was a reaction to the persistent attack from the paparazzi."[8]

As the momentum from her second album wore down, it became time for Lavigne to shift her focus back to creating new music. Actually, she had been doing it all along. While on tour, she would even use her cell phone as a recorder to store guitar parts and melodies when they would pop into her head. At the end of 2006, it was time to see if those phone recordings would translate into another super-popular, multi-platinum, award-winning album. Or would the third time around for Lavigne become less than a charm?

# Career Downs—and Ups

The first new music the public heard from Avril Lavigne in more than two years did not come from the singer's much-anticipated third album. It came from a song she co-wrote for the soundtrack to a movie. "Keep Holding On" was written in 2006 for the fantasy film *Eragon*. Lavigne said she was in the studio working on her upcoming record when she was approached to write a song for the film.

Lavigne said writing for the film provided her with a new test: "This song was specifically written for the movie. It was challenging writing lyrics that had to go exactly with the movie. It was a new experience for me and I learned a lot. I was writing about strength, power, and destiny, while keeping in line with the story of the film."[1]

The plot of that story was based on a book written by Christopher Paolini. It revolves around the adventures of a teenage farm boy and a blue dragon named Saphira. Critics generally gave the film bad reviews. But Lavigne's heartwarming ballad was enjoyed by most who heard it. Released as a single, "Keep Holding On" peaked at number seventeen on *Billboard*'s singles charts. The magazine *Billboard* called it a "gorgeous song."[2] In a note on her official Web site, Lavigne told her fans the song "is no indication of what the rest of [her upcoming] record is like."[3] In truth, it was not. But the song did make it onto the album, once it was released. But before it was, it had to be created and finished.

In the fall of 2006, Lavigne was busy working on her third album. This time, she kept most of the team that had been with her on her second album. Evan Taubenfeld and Butch Walker returned from the *Under My Skin* sessions. However, there was one major addition to the Lavigne team this go-round. His name was Lukasz Gottwald. Known in the business as Dr. Luke, Gottwald was a seasoned guitarist, producer, and songwriter. His resume was star-studded. Prior to working with Lavigne, Gottwald had offered his skills to Kelly Clarkson, Pink, the Veronicas, and many others. He had also co-written "Keep Holding On" with Lavigne. Veteran producer Rob Cavallo, perhaps best known for his work with punk band Green Day, was also on board. So was Lavigne's husband, Deryck Whibley, who played bass and guitar and helped with production, mixing, and other duties. At the beginning of 2007, the work of Lavigne and her team was given a name. The singer's new album was going to be called *The Best Damn Thing*.

Gottwald was a huge addition to the Lavigne team. Including "Keep Holding On," he co-wrote five songs on *The Best Damn Thing*, which now had a release date of mid-April. Two months before the album hit stores, its first single was revealed to the world. It was simply called "Girlfriend." The energetic and rocking tune—written by Lavigne and Gottwald—was an instant hit. The lyrics revolve around a girl who has a crush on a boy who already has a girlfriend. The song features a chanting chorus of "hey"s and "you"s, hand clapping, and even a curse word that had to be censored out for radio airplay. It was a good thing the censoring happened. If it had not, most stations could not have played it. And their doing so is what helped the song reach the top of the charts, as it did in the United States shortly after its release. It was the first number one song of Lavigne's five-year career. "Girlfriend" went to number one in several other countries, as well, including Australia, Ireland, Mexico, and Sweden. It was a big reward for a song Lavigne said the chorus to "was written in two minutes. It took nothing."[4]

Avril Lavigne performs in Beijing, China, while touring in support of her album *The Best Damn Thing*.

With the release of *The Best Damn Thing,* Lavigne's image again changed. This time, she ditched the darker clothing and makeup of her *Under My Skin* years and returned to the happier, more-peppy image she displayed during her *Let Go* era. The music video for "Girlfriend" made the image change clear from the get-go. In it, Lavigne plays three roles: a dorky girlfriend; a rocker girl that wants to be the girlfriend; and herself, wearing black shorts, striped, knee-high socks, high heels, and fishnet stockings. Her hair is blonde with a reddish-pink streak in it. At the end of the video, the rocker girl gets the guy.

**"I got onto the sidewalk and he shot me. It's really cool."**

A picture of Lavigne twirling her streaky hair was the cover of *The Best Damn Thing.* There was an interesting story behind the photo: It was taken by her husband. Lavigne explained, "We got in the car and went to The Valley in [Los Angeles] and I got onto the sidewalk and he shot me. It's a really cool picture. You can pay thousands of dollars to have professionals do this stuff but it was me and Deryck and our two friends who did it all on our computer. I love the cover."[5]

*The Best Damn Thing* hit stores in April. On the strength of its hit single and video—and also Lavigne's own star power—the album debuted at number one on

*Billboard*'s album charts. *The Best Damn Thing* also went to number one in Lavigne's home country of Canada, as well as in Germany, Italy, Japan, Switzerland, the United Kingdom, and elsewhere. As could be expected, Lavigne was thrilled about her accomplishments. She said, "I'm just excited to have the record out and for everyone to hear it now. It's actually number one in fifteen countries, so it's a really exciting time for me. It's crazy."[6] It was about to get crazier for Lavigne. Not all of that craziness was the good kind.

In July—less than three months after *The Best Damn Thing* was released—the Rubinoos, an American pop-rock band from the 1970s and 1980s, sued Lavigne. In 1979, the Rubinoos had released a song called "I Wanna Be Your Boyfriend." They claimed their song was similar to Lavigne's "Girlfriend." So similar, in fact, that they said Lavigne had stolen large parts of their song and used them in hers. Lavigne countered by saying she had never heard of the Rubinoos song, which was written five years before she was born. Those who listened to both songs had varying opinions. Some felt Lavigne had indeed lifted from the Rubinoos. Others felt that the similarities between the two songs were just coincidence. People posted side-by-side comparisons of the song on the Internet video site YouTube and elsewhere online.

There was little denying the songs were indeed similar. The chorus of both songs used the words "hey" and "you" twice. The Rubinoos's song follows those chants with "I wanna be your boyfriend," whereas Lavigne sings, "I don't like your girlfriend." In January 2008, both parties agreed to settle the suit out of court.

Exact terms were not made public, but typical settlements involve the accused party paying money to those who made the accusations. That does not always mean they are admitting guilt. In Lavigne's case, her management said publicly that it would probably be too costly to try and fight the battle in court, so a settlement was the best option. Accurate or not, the Rubinoos's claim damaged Lavigne's reputation as a songwriter. Another accusation that was made against her a month earlier had hurt her just as much. And this one certainly was more personal.

In the June issue of *Performing Artist* magazine, songwriter Chantal Kreviazuk poked fun at Lavigne's songwriting abilities. She said, "I mean, Avril, songwriter? Avril doesn't really sit and write songs by herself. Avril will also cross the ethical line and no one says anything. That's why I'll never work with her again."[7] Kreviazuk had, of course, written songs with Lavigne in the past, including six on Lavigne's second album. Later in the article, Kreviazuk said she had sent Lavigne a song called "Contagious," and then she saw a song with that name on *The Best Damn Thing* but she was not given any credit for writing it.

A few weeks after the article was published, Kreviazuk released a statement apologizing to Lavigne and retracting what she had said about the singer. She did not give an explanation as to why she had made her earlier comments. But by that point, Lavigne's reputation had taken another hit. Kreviazuk's comments already had spread like wildfire around the media circuit, and millions of people had seen them. Lavigne did defend herself against Kreviazuk's accusations. On her blog, Lavigne wrote: "Let it be crystal clear that I have not ripped anyone off or done anything wrong. I have never had to deal with anything publicly like this and surely never wanted to. I do not deserve this negative press and attention. I take pride in the songs that I write and appreciate the opportunities to work with some great writers and musicians."[8]

For the most part, Lavigne escaped both incidents intact. Her reputation was indeed damaged, but the singles and videos from *The Best Damn Thing* continued to be released. The sad "When You're Gone" was released as a single in June. Its accompanying video featured Lavigne playing piano and running through a field, as the clip tells the stories of a woman whose husband left to go to war, and an old man whose wife had recently died. The song made its way onto the charts in several countries, though it fell far short of the successes "Girlfriend" had achieved.

The next single from *The Best Damn Thing* was the spicy "Hot." Like many of Lavigne's songs, it featured lyrics about a girl longing for a boy. The music video followed the same theme as the lyrics. It begins with a dolled-up Lavigne leaving a car to enter a club with the flashing bulbs of cameras all around. She is also a performer in the club, wearing a green and black corset. The final single from the album was its title track, "The Best Damn Thing," a song about convincing a boy that Lavigne is the best thing he has ever seen. The video features Lavigne as a cheerleader, dressed in pink and black.

On average, reviews of *The Best Damn Thing* were about the same as Lavigne's first two albums. Some critics liked it; others did not. *Rolling Stone* magazine gave this one three stars out of five, the same rating it had given her first album, but a half-star less than it had given her second one. However, *The Best Damn Thing* could not match the enormous success of Lavigne's first album either in terms of awards or sales. Not many albums have ever been released that could. But *The Best Damn Thing* did hold its own. Lavigne won several more awards for the album and her performance on it, though she did not win another highly coveted Grammy. *The Best Damn Thing*, like Lavigne's other two albums, has gone platinum in the United States and in several other countries, as well. But it came nowhere near the gigantic sales numbers *Let Go* had achieved.

In the midst of promoting her latest album and dealing with the controversy surrounding it, Lavigne still found

Children in rags rest in an open-air makeshift camp after escaping an attack that left forty others dead in Sudan's Darfur province in 2006.

time to continue her charity work. In June 2007, her version of John Lennon's classic song of peace and hope, "Imagine," was released on a double album called *Make Some Noise: The Amnesty International Campaign to Save Darfur*.

Darfur is a section of the northeastern Africa country of Sudan engaged in a civil war. Tens of thousands—possibly hundreds of thousands—of people have died because of the human rights and humanitarian crisis. The release featured bands such as Aerosmith, Green Day, R.E.M., U2, and others covering Lennon songs. Sales of *Make Some Noise* raised more than $2.5 million for the cause.

In November, Lavigne headlined the Unite Against AIDS concert in Montreal, Quebec, Canada. The show benefited UNICEF's Unite for Children, Unite Against AIDS campaign. The next month, Lavigne signed an acoustic and an electric guitar for the Starlight Children's Foundation, an organization that helps seriously ill children and their families.

Lavigne spent a majority of 2007 promoting her album on popular TV shows and at select public appearances. But the majority of fans wanting to see Lavigne perform her new songs, and her old ones, live had to wait until nearly a year after *The Best Damn Thing* was released. At the end of 2007, Lavigne finally announced the details of her Best Damn Tour. The tour was to open March 5,

2008, in Victoria, British Columbia, and travel all across Canada, the United States, and most of Europe.

Lavigne was excited about hitting the road again. And this tour was to be bigger and better than ever. She said: "We finally get to go out [on tour] after a year of promo, a lot of hard work, so I'm excited to go out and play live. There's gonna be dancing; it's going to be really upbeat. I'm taking my show to the next level. It's still gonna be very me, and rock-influenced . . . but it's also gonna be diverse. It's going to open with a bang and dancers, and in the middle of the set [we're] coming down and doing acoustic stuff and me performing by myself."[9] She told one interviewer that her being around longer will help make for a better show. She said, "Being that it's my third album, I feel like I'm a lot better now. And I've got, like, ten singles to play now, which makes it so much easier and so much better. When you play the hits onstage, it's the most exciting part of the show. And I have more to work with now. . . . It's definitely not going to be boring."[10]

The theme of The Best Damn Tour was the color pink, and the opening act was a pop-rock band from Boston called Boys Like Girls. Everyone involved with the tour was excited to get started. Lavigne was too. From the hundreds of messages from fans on her Web site, it appeared she was not the only one.

# A Happy Ending?

By the time 2008 rolled around, Lavigne was much more than just a musician. In the six years since the release of her first album, the twenty-three-year-old had evolved into an all-around entertainer: actress, model, singer, and wife. To this day, her list of accomplishments continues to grow.

In 2007, Lavigne was made into a character in a series of comic books called *Avril Lavigne's Make 5 Wishes*. The books are created in the Japanese manga style, and are about a lonely teenage girl named Hana, whose best friend is an imaginary Avril Lavigne. In July 2008, Lavigne even became a clothing designer. She teamed up with the American department store chain Kohl's to produce a line of clothing called Abbey Dawn. Abbey Dawn was the nickname Lavigne's father called her when she was young. The affordable clothing line features several styles and prints Lavigne has been known to wear, including checkers, skulls, stars, and more, on hoodies, skinny jeans, skirts, and other items. Lavigne told one magazine how excited she was for her clothing line, and how the designing process works. She said, "I am the designer and the concept obviously came from me. As far as designing goes, I just sat down and told everyone what I love and what I don't like, and basically the clothes are everything that I would wear."[1]

As expected, thousands of fans turned out for each show on The Best Damn Tour. But ticket sales were slow, at times, and not all shows were sold out, as they had been in the past. When asked about the troubles some places have had selling tickets for her show, Lavigne had an explanation. She said, "I've done about 23 shows in five weeks and I've sold 170,000, I'm on top of that stuff. Of course you're gonna have a show that doesn't sell out. Especially when they put me in a 20,000-seater and I'm only selling 10,000 tickets. Venues are so big. 'Cause it's the one available or whatever."[2]

Those who attended were greeted with the most well-rounded show Lavigne had ever staged. There was a new band backing her up, dancers on a couple of songs, a pink-and-black checkered stage with a large skull and crossbones in the middle. Lavigne even played a pink guitar and sang into a microphone that rests in a pink stand. For the most part, the tour sailed along smoothly.

In addition to sluggish ticket sales, there were two other noteworthy bumps that occurred during The Best Damn Tour. The first began at the end of April. After performing in Las Vegas, Lavigne had to cancel several shows due to acute laryngitis. Some suggested her sickness was a result of her partying the night away in Las Vegas. The singer gave her explanation on her Web site: "I have been sick this whole tour, and now I have lost my voice. I have never canceled a show in my whole career and just had to for the first time ever. This sux! I am so sorry! I have been on the road for 60 days straight. . . . I think I am just run down. I just played 4 shows in a row in Texas (which is a lot for the vocals) and woke up in Vegas Tuesday with no voice. I thought I was gonna have to cancel that show, but I made it through . . . barely!"[3]

Months later, she also was "barely" able to perform at her scheduled show in the Southeast Asia country of Malaysia. One religious group there asked the government not to allow the concert to take place. The group's leader said, "It is considered too sexy for us . . . it's not good for viewers in Malaysia. We don't want our people, our teenagers, influenced by their performance. We want clean artists, artists that are good role models."[4] The

Avril Lavigne presents her new clothing line Abbey Dawn in Tokyo, Japan, on September 14, 2008.

show was temporarily canceled but eventually went on as scheduled.

Tabloid magazines frequently had reported that Lavigne's marriage to Deryck Whibley was about to end in divorce. In the past, every time one of those types of rumors popped up, either Lavigne or Whibley released a statement denying it was true. Unfortunately, in 2009, Lavigne's Web site had announced that she and her husband were, in fact, separating. About the rumors she constantly reads about herself, Lavigne said: "Yeah of course, as a human it can be hurtful, but at the same time I don't let it affect me because there are more positives going on than negatives."[5]

Rumors of Lavigne being pregnant also frequently pop up. Those are consistently denied. On that subject, Lavigne told a magazine, "Oh God! I don't want to have kids for like ten years. I still have a lot to do. I don't even know if I could handle a dog right now. I'm *so* not ready. Someday I'll be a mom but not until I'm in my 30s."[6] Lavigne and Whibley did have fun with those persistent pregnancy rumors. In the beginning of 2008, she padded her stomach and went with her husband into a store in a popular area of Los Angeles to look at baby clothes. Soon, stories were all over the Internet, saying Lavigne was pregnant. A few years earlier, Lavigne even called her mother as a joke on April Fool's Day to tell her she was pregnant.

However, some of the negative news reported about Lavigne's career actually proved to be true. When sales of *The Best Damn Thing* and ticket sales for The Best Damn Tour failed to meet expectations, reports began surfacing that Lavigne and her management company soon might part ways. In December 2008, they did. Lavigne fired longtime manager Terry McBride of Nettwerk, and replaced him with Irving Azoff. Azoff has worked with some of the industry's biggest names, including Jewel, the Eagles, Van Halen, Guns N' Roses, and Christina Aguilera. Time will tell how he will work out for Lavigne.

The disappointing sales of *The Best Damn Thing* may have caused her to fire her manager, but "disappointing" is a relative term. Lavigne's third album still sold more than 5 million copies worldwide. Her second album, *Under My Skin,* has sold more than 8 million copies to date. Lavigne's triumphant debut, *Let Go,* has sold more than 16 million copies. That is roughly 30 million records at age twenty-four. Today, Lavigne is a multimillionaire, and is consistently included on magazine's "richest celebrity" lists. Considering all the products that are associated with Lavigne's name, it is likely she will stay there for a long time. She could even go higher on the lists than she has, if her acting career pans out. In 2010, Lavigne sang a song called "Alice" for the soundtrack to the film, *Alice in Wonderland*, appeared as a judge in the early rounds of the TV show *American Idol*, and performed at the Winter Olympics in Vancouver, Canada.

Exactly what the future holds for Lavigne is anybody's guess. Will she continue to release platinum albums every two or three years? Will she become a successful actress and win awards in that discipline? Or will her young fans grow up and move on from their rebellious idol?

Several industry insiders have, for years, predicted Lavigne's demise, but it has not yet happened. Lavigne's former songwriter Cliff Magness believes it likely never

Avril Lavigne poses with children in Beijing, China, as part of a charity event prior to her solo concert there on October 6, 2008.

will. He thinks Lavigne has what it takes to become a career artist. He said, "Avril has always seemed like an old soul to me. She also has been careful not to show all of her cards. Still waters run deep, ya know? But I think if there is anything to be attributed to her longevity, it would be her drive and her ambition. And of course, her talent. Without the former two, the latter is irrelevant. She's had three multi-platinum albums, and acting and fashion success."[7]

A big part of Lavigne's appeal always has been her life story. When a young girl from a small town in Canada becomes one of the biggest stars on the planet, people everywhere get inspired. But when that small-town girl becomes successful, negative people everywhere begin looking for flaws. Sometimes, they even find them. But in spite of all the negativity Lavigne has had to endure, she constantly has said that underneath all the hype, rumors, and successes, she remains that same small-town girl she always was—the one who loved to stand on her bed and sing, pretending thousands of people were hearing her gifted voice, when no one actually was. "I'm just some chick from Napanee, Ontario," she said, "and I can't believe where I am today."[8]

# Chronology

**1984**—Avril Ramona Lavigne born September 27 in Belleville, Ontario, Canada, to John and Judy Lavigne.

**1989**—Moves with family to Napanee, Ontario.

**1991**—First public singing performance, as member of church choir.

**1994**—Enters Cornerstone Christian Academy.

**1996**—Plays role of Sally in a community theatre production of *You're a Good Man, Charlie Brown*.

**1998**—Sings at the Quinte Spirit Festival.

**1999**—Sings on Stephen Medd's *Quinte Spirit*; wins radio station contest; shares stage with country star Shania Twain; meets future manager Cliff Fabri.

**2000**—Sings on Medd's *My Window to You*; signs record deal with Arista Records; drops out of high school and moves to New York, then Los Angeles.

**2002**—Debut album, *Let Go,* released, sells more than 8 million copies worldwide; plays herself in episode of *Sabrina, The Teenage Witch*.

**2003**—Performs on *Saturday Night Live*; nominated for five Grammy Awards; wins four Juno Awards; featured on the cover of *Rolling Stone*; takes part in several charity events.

**2004**—Releases *Under My Skin* album; performs in front of England's Prince Charles at Party in the Park charity event in London; records own version of *SpongeBob SquarePants* theme song.

**2005**—Appears on cover of *Cosmopolitan*; gets engaged to Sum 41's Deryck Whibley; wins three more Juno Awards.

**2006**—Weds Whibley; performs at Winter Olympics in Italy; writes song for film *Eragon*.

**2007**—Releases *The Best Damn Thing*; records John Lennon's "Imagine" for charity album; sued by band claiming she stole large parts of one of their songs for use in her song "Girlfriend"; becomes character in series of comic books called *Avril Lavigne's Make 5 Wishes*.

**2008**—Settles out of court on "Girlfriend" lawsuit; starts own clothing line, Abbey Dawn; travels world for her The Best Damn Tour.

**2009**—Lavigne's Web site announces that she and Whibley are separating.

**2010**—Performs at Winter Olympics; contributes song to *Alice in Wonderland* soundtrack; appears as celebrity judge on *American Idol*.

# Discography

**Albums**

**2002**—*Let Go*

**2004**—*Under My Skin*

**2007**—*The Best Damn Thing*

**Singles**

**2002**—"Complicated"

"Sk8er Boi"

**2003**—"I'm With You"

"Losing Grip"

**2004**—"Mobile"

"Don't Tell Me"

"My Happy Ending"

"Nobody's Home"

**2005**—"He Wasn't"

**2007**—"Girlfriend"

"When You're Gone

**2008**—"The Best Damn Thing"

## Songs on Compilations

**2003**—"Knockin' on Heaven's Door," *War Child: Hope*

**2004**—"SpongeBob SquarePants Theme," *The SpongeBob SquarePants Movie: Music From the Movie and More*

**2006**—"Keep Holding On," *Eragon*

**2007**—"Imagine," *Instant Karma: The Amnesty International Campaign to Save Darfur*

**2010**—"Alice," *Almost Alice, the Alice in Wonderland soundtrack*

# Chapter Notes

## Chapter 1.
### A Royal Performance

1. "Lavigne and Prince Harry Romance on the Cards?" *ContactMusic.com,* April 26, 2004, <http://www.contactmusic.com/new/xmlfeed.nsf/story/lavigne-and-prince-harry-romance-on-the-cards> (November 20, 2008).

2. Ibid.

3. Gordon Smart, "Mean Lavigne Snubs Charles," *Sun,* July 12, 2004, <http://www.thesun.co.uk/sol/homepage/showbiz/bizarre/article209706.ece> (November 10, 2008).

4. "Avril Poops Party," *Yahoo! Music News UK and Ireland,* July 12, 2004, <http://uk.news.launch.yahoo.com/dyna/article.html?a=/040712/340/ext93.html&e=l_news_dm> (November 10, 2008).

5. Smart.

6. Avril Lavigne, "Party in the Park Interview," *YouTube,* 2004, <http://www.youtube.com/watch?v=MGB95RNKnmg> (October 16, 2008).

7. Ibid.

## Chapter 2.
### She Was a Sk8er Girl

1. Jenny Eliscu, "Little Miss Can't Be Wrong," *Rolling Stone,* March 20, 2003, <http://www.rollingstone.com/news/coverstory/avril_lavigne_five_feet_one/page/2> (October 15, 2008).

2. Ibid.

3. "2002 Biography," *ALavigne.com,* n.d., <http://www.alavi-gne.com/information/avril-lavigne-bio.php> (October 12, 2008).

4. David Segal, "Avril Lavigne, Unvarnished," *TeenMusic.com,* January 14, 2003, <http://www.teenmusic.com/d.asp?r=27426&p=4> (November 12, 2008).

5. Chris Willman, "Avril Lavigne: The Anti-Britney," *Entertainment Weekly,* November 1, 2002, <http://www.ew.com/ew/article/0,,384096_3,00.htm> (November 10, 2008).

6. Shanda Deziel, "Avril's Edge," *Maclean's,* January 13, 2003, reproduced at the *Canadian Encyclopedia,* 2009, <http://www.thecanadianencyclopedia.com/index.cfm?PgNm=TCE&Params=M1ARTM0012431> (October 10, 2008).

7. Willman.

8. Ann Marie McQueen, "Avril's Wild Ride to Stardom," *Ottawa Sun,* February 9, 2003, reproduced at *Canoe—Jam!* n.d., <http://jam.canoe.ca/Music/Artists/L/Lavigne_Avril/2003/02/09/746834.html> (November 14, 2008).

9. Paul Cantin, "The Real Lavigne, Behind Ontario's Pop-punk Princess Lurks a Not-so-wild Past," *Toronto Star,* August 27, 2002, reproduced at *RomanLine Productions,* n.d., <http://www.romanline.com/press_tstar.html> (October 10, 2008).

10. Willman.

11. "Growing up Avril (The True Story)," *YouTube,* December 10, 2007, <http://www.youtube.com/watch?v=IcLKxherTOs> (November 10, 2008).

12. Willman.

13. Ibid.

14. Edmund J. Lee, "What She Wants Is What She Gets," *New York Times,* November 24, 2002, <http://query.nytimes.com/gst/fullpage.html?res=9806E1DB1F30F937A15752C1A9649C8B63> (October 12, 2008).

15. Ibid.

16. Eliscu, <http://www.rollingstone.com/news/coverstory/avril_lavigne_five_feet_one/page/>.

17. Marc Guarino, "A 'More Confident' Avril Lavigne Puts More Energy Into Her Show," *Daily Herald,* March 21, 2008, <http://www.dailyherald.com/story/?id=156489> (November 12, 2008).

## Chapter 3.
## Take Me Away

1. Paul Cantin, "The Real Lavigne, Behind Ontario's Pop-punk Princess Lurks a Not-so-wild Past," *Toronto Star,* August 27, 2002, reproduced at *RomanLine Productions,* n.d., <http://www.romanline.com/press_tstar.html> (October 10, 2008).

2. Jenny Eliscu, "Little Miss Can't Be Wrong," *Rolling Stone,* March 20, 2003, <http://www.rollingstone.com/news/coverstory/avril_lavigne_five_feet_one/page/> (October 15, 2008).

3. "Avril Lavigne: Record Deal," *A&E's Private Sessions,* n.d., <http://link.biography.com/services/link/bcpid1740037445/bctid1723556677> (November 12, 2008).

4. Eliscu.

5. Ann Marie McQueen, "Avril's Wild Ride to Stardom," *Ottawa Sun,* February 9, 2003, reproduced at *Canoe—Jam!* n.d., <http://jam.canoe.ca/Music/Artists/L/Lavigne_Avril/2003/02/09/746834.html> (November 14, 2008).

6. Marianne Beattie, "Life's Like This," *Faze,* Fall 2002, <http://www.fazeteen.com/fall2002/avrillavigne.htm> (October 17, 2008).

7. Personal interview with Cliff Magness, November 11, 2008.

8. Ibid.

9. Ibid.

10. Chris Willman, "Avril Lavigne: The Anti-Britney," *Entertainment Weekly,* November 1, 2002, <http://www.ew.com/ew/article/0,,384096_3,00.htm> (November 10, 2008).

11. David Segal, "Avril Lavigne, Unvarnished," *TeenMusic.com,* January 14, 2003, <http://www.teenmusic.com/d.asp?r=27426&p=4> (November 12, 2008).

12. Willman.

13. Eliscu.

14. Shirley Halperin, "Spotlight On . . . Avril Lavigne," *Entertainment Weekly,* April 13, 2007, <http://www.ew.com/ew/article/0,,20033891,00.html> (September 12, 2008).

## Chapter 4.

## Her World

1. Heather Stas, "Avril Lavigne: Too Much Too Young," *VH1.com,* July 11, 2002, <http://www.vh1.com/artists/news/1456027/07112002/lavigne_avril.jhtml> (September 23, 2008).

2. "Avril Uncensored," *Cosmopolitan,* n.d., <http://www.cosmopolitan.com/celebrities/exclusive/avril-lavigne-2> (October 24, 2008).

3. "Avril Lavigne: In Her Own Words," *People.com,* April 13, 2007, <http://www.people.com/people/gallery/0,,20034335_20047784,00.html/#20047787> (November 12, 2008).

4. Elysa Gardner, "Avril Lavigne Skates Straight to the Top," *USA Today,* July 7, 2002, <http://www.usatoday.com/life/music/2002/2002-07-10-avril.htm> (October 10, 2008).

5. Gil Kaufman, "Avril Lavigne—Fashion Rebel With A (Good) Cause," *MTV.com,* March 10, 2003, <http://www.mtv.com/news/articles/1470449/20030310/lavigne_avril.jhtml?headlines= true> (November 11, 2008).

6. Edmund J. Lee, "What She Wants Is What She Gets," *New York Times,* November 24, 2002, <http://query.nytimes.com/gst/fullpage.html?res=9806E1DB1F30F937A15752C1A9649C8B63> (October 12, 2008).

7. Avril Lavigne, "Losing Grip (Juno Awards 2003)," *YouTube,* September 12, 2007, <http://www.youtube.com/watch?v=IFWQYr6eeis> (October 12, 2008).

8. Ibid.

9. Corey Moss and SuChin Pak, "Avril Lavigne Writing Next LP, Yearns For The Open Road," *MTV.com,* September 4, 2002, <http://www.mtv.com/news/articles/1457302/20020903/lavigne_avril.jhtml> (September 2, 2008).

## Chapter 5.
### Celebrity Pros and Cons

1. Jon Wiederhorn, "Avril and Fred Durst Make Beautiful Music Together," *MTV.com,* May 19, 2003, <http://www.mtv.com/news/articles/1471958/20030519/lavigne_avril.jhtml> (September 12, 2008).

2. Austin Scaggs, "Q&A: Avril in Action," *Rolling Stone,* June 3, 2004, <http://www.rollingstone.com/artists/avrillavigne/articles/story/6085406/qa_avril_in_action> (September 12, 2008).

3. Jennifer Sullivan, "Man Charged With Stalking Singer Lavigne," *Seattle Times,* August 28, 2004, <http://seattletimes.nwsource.com/html/localnews/2002018375_avril28m.html> (October 16, 2008).

4. Jim Haley, "Lynnwood Stalker Sentenced to 30 Days," *Herald* (Everett, WA), April 30, 2005, <http://www.heraldnet.com/article/20050430/NEWS01/504300719&SearchID=73337231976259> (November 25, 2008).

5. Ibid.

6. "Skin Is In," *Billboard,* May 23, 2004, <http://www.billboard.com/bbcom/esearch/article_display.jsp?vnu_content_id=1000517308> (October 12, 2008).

7. Karen Bliss, "Avril Lavigne's Dark Side," *Rolling Stone,* April 1, 2004, <http://www.rollingstone.com/artists/chantalkreviazuk/articles/story/5936982/avril_lavignes_dark_side> (October 14, 2008).

8. Personal interview with Cliff Magness, November 11, 2008.

9. "Skin Is In."

## Chapter 6.

## On the Road Again

1. Edna Gunderson, "Buyers Are Big on Lavigne, Even If Radio Isn't," *USA Today,* June 2, 2004, <http://www.usatoday.com/life/music/news/2004-06-02-lavigne-album_x.htm> (October 15, 2008).

2. "Avril Gets Rude on MTV," *ContactMusic.com,* May 20, 2004, <http://www.contactmusic.com/new/xmlfeed.nsf/story/avril-gets-rude-on-mtv#> (October 28, 2009).

3. Kelefa Sanneh, "Avril Lavigne: Under My Skin," *Rolling Stone,* June 10, 2004, <http://www.rollingstone.com/artists/avrillavigne/albums/album/6041348/review/6054703/under_my_skin> (October 15, 2008).

4. Joe D'Angelo, "Avril Lavigne: No Looking Back," *MTV.com,* March 22, 2004, <http://www.mtv.com/bands/l/lavigne_avril/news_feature_032204/index.jhtml> (November 12, 2008).

5. Carolyn E. Davis, "Avril Lavigne Will Play the Hits She Hates For Fans," *MTV.com,* March 25, 2005, <http://www.mtv.com/news/articles/1499071/20050325/ lavigne_avril.jhtml?headlines=true> (October 27, 2008).

6. Dan Aquilante, "Don't Give Avril Any Lip: Lavigne Tells Syncher Simpson to Get Real!" *New York Post,* November 7, 2004, p. 91, <http://www.nypost.com/p/entertainment/real_give_avril_any_lip_lavigne_cWjoNO66Oqt7obP5V42NzL> (October 9, 2009).

7. Ibid.

8. Jeanette Walls, "Britney Spears Gets Scolding From Avril Lavigne," *MSNBC,* May 12, 2004, <http://www.msnbc.msn.com/ID/4954240/?> (October 12, 2008).

9. Ibid.

10. Joe D'Angelo, "Avril Lavigne Gives Squishy SpongeBob Song A Harder Edge," *MTV.com,* November 4, 2004, <http://www.mtv.com/news/articles/1493449/20041104/lavigne_avril.jhtml> (November 14, 2008).

## Chapter 7.
## Branching Out

1. Jenny Eliscu, "Little Miss Can't Be Wrong," *Rolling Stone,* March 20, 2003, <http://www.rollingstone.com/news/coverstory/avril_lavigne_five_feet_one/page/4> (October 25, 2008).

2. Ibid.

3. "Avril Lavigne: In Her Own Words," *People.com,* April 13, 2007, <http://www.people.com/people/gallery/0,,20034335_20047784,00.html/#20047787> (November 12, 2008).

4. Ibid.

5. Nekesa Mumbi Moody, "Q&A with Avril Lavigne," *Post-Gazette* (Pittsburgh), April 19, 2007, <http://www.post-gazette.com/pg/07119/781377-42.stm> (October 18, 2008).

6. "Lavigne Wants High-End Modeling Gig," *San Francisco Chronicle,* January 24, 2006, <http://www.sfgate.com/cgi-bin/blogs/sfgate/detail?blogid=7&entry_id=2689> (October 18, 2008).

7. Ibid.

8. Bill Harris, "Avril Sorry for Spitting, Swearing," *Toronto Sun,* September 30, 2006, *Jam—Canoe!* n.d., <http://jam.canoe.ca/Music/Artists/L/Lavigne_Avril/2006/09/30/1924447.html> (November 15, 2008).

## Chapter 8.
## Career Downs–and Ups

1. Avril Lavigne, "Hey Guys," *AvrilLavigne.com,* November 8, 2006, <http://www.avrillavigne.com/node/236> (November 12, 2008).

2. Chuck Taylor, "Avril Lavigne: Keep Holding On," *Billboard,* December 2, 2006, <http://www.billboard.com/bbcom/reviews/single_review_display.jsp?vnu_content_id=1003437971> (November 12, 2008).

3. Lavigne.

4. Jennifer Vineyard, "Don't Know How To Spell 'Avril Lavigne'? Prepare To Be Scolded," *MTV.com,* February 28, 2007, <http://www.mtv.com/news/articles/1553431/20070227/lavigne_avril.jhtml> (October 20, 2008).

5. "Avril Lavigne Shoots Own Album Cover With Husband," *Starpulse.com,* April 16, 2007, <http://www.starpulse.com/news/index.php/2007/04/16/avril_lavigne_shoots_own_album_cover_wit> (October 28, 2008).

6. "Avril Lavigne Happy Atop Pop Charts," *UPI,* May 1, 2007, <http://www.upi.com/Entertainment_News/2007/05/01/Avril_Lavigne_happy_atop_pop_charts/UPI-70141178024072/> (November 12, 2008).

7. Bob Cannon, "Chantal Kreviazuk," *Performing Songwriter,* June 2007, pp. 67–68.

8. Athima Chansanchai, "Lavigne Is Under Fire Again," *Seattle Post-Intelligencer,* July 9, 2007, <http://seattlepi.nwsource.com/people/322977_people10.html> (October 12, 2008).

9. James Montgomery, "Avril Lavigne Promises 2008 Jaunt Will Be Her Best Damn Tour Yet," *MTV.com,* November 7, 2007, <http://www.mtv.com/news/articles/1573708/20071107/lavigne_avril.jhtml> (October 19, 2008).

10. Ibid.

## Chapter 9.
## A Happy Ending?

1. John Warech, "OK! Interview: Avril Lavigne," *OK! Magazine,* July 30, 2008, <http://www.okmagazine.com/news/view/8095> (October 15, 2008).

2. Shannon Breen, "The Sk8er Girl vs. the H8ers," *St. Petersburg Times,* April 18, 2008, p. 38.

3. Avril Lavigne, "Message From Avril," *AvrilLavigne.com,* May 1, 2008, <http://www.avrillavigne.com/node/7382> (October 15, 2008).

4. Josh Grossberg, "Avril 'Too Sexy' For Malaysia?," *E! Online,* August 18, 2008, <http://www.eonline.com/uberblog/detail.jsp?contentId=24282> (October 19, 2008).

5. Warech.

6. Ibid.

7. Personal interview with Cliff Magness, November 11, 2008.

8. Warech.

# Further Reading

Jay, Natasha. *Avril Lavigne: She's Complicated*. New York: Icon Press, 2006.

Tracy, Kathleen. *Avril Lavigne*. Hockessin, Del.: Mitchell Lane, 2005.

Ventresca, Yvonne. *Avril Lavigne*. Detroit: Lucent, 2007.

Watson, Galadriel. *Avril Lavigne*. Calgary, Alberta, Canada: Weigl Educational Publishers, 2007.

## Internet Addresses

**Avril Lavigne Official Site**
   http://www.avrillavigne.com/

**ALavigne.com**
   http://www.alavigne.com/

# Index